CW00724356

Gillian A. Dunne
Editor

Living "Difference": Lesbian Perspectives on Work and Family Life

Living "Difference": Lesbian Perspectives on Work and Family Life has been co-published simultaneously as *Journal of Lesbian Studies,* Volume 2, Number 4 1998.

Pre-publication
REVIEWS,
COMMENTARIES,
EVALUATIONS . . .

"This is a fascinating, ground-breaking collection of articles on the impact of sexual identity on people's experience of work and family life. Gillian Dunne presents a brilliant analysis of an egalitarian approach to parenting, domestic and employment responsibilities in lesbian families as a model for heterosexual couples. Students and professionals in psychiatry, psychology, sociology, and anthropology will find this work extremely useful and thought-provoking."

Nanette K. Gartrell, MD
Associate Clinical Professor of Psychiatry
University of California
San Francisco Medical School

Harrington Park Press

Living "Difference":
Lesbian Persectives
on Work and Family Life

Living "Difference": Lesbian Perspectives on Work and Family Life has been co-published simultaneously as *Journal of Lesbian Studies,* Volume 2, Number 4 1998.

Living "Difference": Lesbian Perspectives on Work and Family Life

Gillian A. Dunne, PhD
Editor

Living "Difference": Lesbian Perspectives on Work and Family Life, edited by Gillian A. Dunne, was simultaneously issued by The Haworth Press, Inc., under the same title, as a special issue of the *Journal of Lesbian Studies,* Volume 2, Number 4, 1998, Esther D. Rothblum, Editor.

Harrington Park Press
An Imprint of
The Haworth Press, Inc.
New York • London

ISBN 1-56023-115-7

Living "Difference": Lesbian Perspectives on Work and Family Life has been co-published simultaneously as *Journal of Lesbian Studies*™, Volume 2, Number 4 1998.

The development, preparation, and publication of this work has been undertaken with great care. However, the publisher, employees, editors, and agents of The Haworth Press and all imprints of The Haworth Press, Inc., including The Haworth Medical Press® and Pharmaceutical Products Press®, are not responsible for any errors contained herein or for consequences that may ensue from use of materials or information contained in this work. Opinions expressed by the author(s) are not necessarily those of The Haworth Press, Inc.

Library of Congress Cataloging-in-Publication Data

Living "difference" : lesbian perspectives on work and family life / Gillian A. Dunne, editor.
     p. cm.
   Co-published simultaneously as Journal of lesbian studies, Volume 2, Number 4, 1998.
   Includes bibliographical references (p.   ) and index.
   ISBN 0-7890-0537-9 (alk. paper). – ISBN 1-56023-115-7 (alk. paper)
    1. Lesbian mothers. 2. Gay parents. I. Dunne, Gillian A. II. Journal of lesbian studies, v. 2, no. 4.
HQ75.53.L58   1998
306.874'3'086643–dc21   98-38652
                                                                        CIP

INDEXING & ABSTRACTING

Contributions to this publication are selectively indexed or abstracted in print, electronic, online, or CD-ROM version(s) of the reference tools and information services listed below. This list is current as of the copyright date of this publication. See the end of this section for additional notes.

- *Abstracts in Social Gerontology: Current Literature on Aging,* National Council on the Aging, Library, 409 Third Street SW, 2nd Floor, Washington, DC 20024

- *CNPIEC Reference Guide: Chinese National Directory of Foreign Periodicals*, P.O. Box 88, Beijing, People's Republic of China

- *Contemporary Wopmen's Issues,* Resposive Databases Services, 23611 Chagrin Boulevard, Suite 320, Beachwood, OH 44122

- *Feminist Periodicals: A Current Listing of Contents,* Women's Studies Librarian-at-Large, 728 State Street, 430 Memorial Library, Madison, WI 53706

- *Gay & Lesbian Abstracts,* National Information Services Corporation, 306 East Baltimore Pike, 2nd Floor, Media, PA 19063

- *HOMODOK/"Relevant" Bibliographic database, Documentation Centre for Gay & Lesbian Studies, University of Amsterdam (selective printed abstracts in "Homologie" and bibliographic computer databases covering cultural, historical, social and political aspects of gay & lesbian topics)*, HOMODOK-ILGA Archive, O.Z. Achterburgwal 185, NL-1012 DK Amsterdam, The Netherlands

- *Index to Periodical Articles Related to Law,* University of Texas, 727 East 26th Street, Austin, TX 78705

(continued)

- *INTERNET ACCESS (& additional networks) Bulletin Board for Libraries ("BUBL") coverage of information resources on INTERNET, JANET, and other networks.*
  - <URL:http://bubl.ac.uk/>
  - The new locations will be found under <URL:http://bubl.ac.uk/link/>.
  - Any existing BUBL users who have problems finding information on the new service should contact the BUBL help line by sending e-mail to <bubl@bubl.ac.uk>.
  The Andersonian Library, Curran Building, 101 St. James Road, Glasgow G4 0NS, Scotland

- *PAIS Bulletin,* Public Affairs Information Service, Inc., 521 West 43rd Street, New York, NY 10036-4396

- *Referativnyi Zhurnal (Abstracts Journal of the All-Russian Institute of Scientific and Technical Information),* 20 Usievich Street, Moscow 125219, Russia

- *Sociological Abstracts (SA),* Sociological Abstracts, Inc., P.O. Box 22206, San Diego, CA 92192-0206

- *Studies on Women Abstracts,* Carfax Publishing Company, P.O. Box 25, Abingdon, Oxon OX14 3UE United Kingdom

- *Women "R" CD/ROM,* Softline Information, Inc., 20 Summer Street, Stamford, CT 06901. A new full text Windows Database on CD/ROM. Presents full depth coverage of the wide range of subjects that impact and reflect the lives of women. Can be reached at 1 (800) 524-7922, www.slinfo.com, or e-mail: hoch@slinfo.com

- *Women's Studies Index (indexed comprehensively),* G.K. Hall & Co., P. O. Box 159, Thorndike, ME 04986

(continued)

SPECIAL BIBLIOGRAPHIC NOTES

related to special journal issues (separates)
and indexing/abstracting

❏ indexing/abstracting services in this list will also cover material in any "separate" that is co-published simultaneously with Haworth's special thematic journal issue or DocuSerial. Indexing/abstracting usually covers material at the article/chapter level.

❏ monographic co-editions are intended for either non-subscribers or libraries which intend to purchase a second copy for their circulating collections.

❏ monographic co-editions are reported to all jobbers/wholesalers/approval plans. The source journal is listed as the "series" to assist the prevention of duplicate purchasing in the same manner utilized for books-in-series.

❏ to facilitate user/access services all indexing/abstracting services are encouraged to utilize the co-indexing entry note indicated at the bottom of the first page of each article/chapter/contribution.

❏ this is intended to assist a library user of any reference tool (whether print, electronic, online, or CD-ROM) to locate the monographic version if the library has purchased this version but not a subscription to the source journal.

❏ individual articles/chapters in any Haworth publication are also available through the Haworth Document Delivery Service (HDDS).

ABOUT THE EDITOR

Gillian A. Dunne, PhD, is a Senior Research Fellow at The Gender Institute of The London School of Economics and a former Senior Research Associate in the Faculty of Social and Political Sciences at Cambridge University. Her research interests focus on key feminist and sociological issues through the experiences of lesbian women. For the past three years, Dr. Dunne has been researching lesbian couples with dependent children. She is currently studying the different dimensions of gay fatherhood. In addition, Dr. Dunne is the author of the book *Lesbian Lifestyles: Women's Work and the Politics of Sexuality* (1997).

CONTENTS

Introduction:
Add Sexuality and Stir:
Towards a Broader Understanding
of the Gender Dynamics
# of Work and Family Life

Gillian A. Dunne

Such has been the impact of feminism on intellectual thought over the past twenty years that it would be a brave and foolhardy social scientist who could discuss the organization of work and family life, without reference to gender. The addition of gender into the analysis, while a source of irritation for more conventional thinkers in the past, can now be acknowledged as generating better understandings of change and continuity in the home and in the workplace.

There remains, however, a further intellectual blind spot in dominant accounts. This has been sustained by a lack of curiosity about

The author is extremely grateful to the following for their encouragement, friendship and insightful comments: Shirley Prendergast, Ginny Morrow, Andrea Doucet, Wendy Bottero. The project on lesbian parents was made possible through a grant from the Economic and Social Research Council (reference R00023 4649). She would also like to thank her co-applicants–Henrietta Moore and Bob Blackburn, and those poorly paid but highly valued others who have assisted her on the project–Kim Perrin, Esther Dermott and Jackie Beer.

[Haworth co-indexing entry note]: "Introduction: Add Sexuality and Stir: Towards a Broader Understanding of the Gender Dynamics of Work and Family Life." Dunne, Gillian A. Co-published simultaneously in *Journal of Lesbian Studies* (The Haworth Press, Inc.) Vol. 2, No. 4, 1998, pp. 1-8; and: *Living "Difference": Lesbian Perspectives on Work and Family Life* (ed: Gillian A. Dunne) The Haworth Press, Inc., 1998, pp. 1-8; and: *Living "Difference": Lesbian Perspectives on Work and Family Life* (ed: Gillian A. Dunne) Harrington Park Press, an imprint of The Haworth Press, Inc., 1998, pp. 1-8. Single or multiple copies of this article are available for a fee from The Haworth Document Delivery Service [1-800-342-9678, 9:00 a.m. - 5:00 p.m. (EST). E-mail address: getinfo@haworthpressinc.com].

1

the impact of sexual identity on people's experience of work and family life. Mainstream feminist thinking about the limitations and possibilities for transformation in the gender order is informed by empirical research which perpetuates an assumption that workers, parents, and households are heterosexual. Just as the tendency to conflate the category 'worker' with 'man' distorted and obscured understanding, this heterosexual framework limits our capacity to identify obstacles to the creation of a more egalitarian relationship between the sexes. For example, it conceals the significance of heterosexuality *itself* for shaping the lifechances of women and men. I argue that non-heterosexual experience provides important comparative reference points which can tell us as much about heterosexuality, gender, gender relations, and the mainstream as they do about anything else.

The contributions in this volume upset conventional understandings of work and family life by challenging many of the implicit assumptions that have anchored previous research. The issues explored in each essay demonstrate the need to bring the study of lesbian experience from the margins to the centre of feminist enquiry. In this introduction I shall briefly illustrate why better accounts can be produced by adding sexuality and stirring by focusing on two research projects that I have conducted. My conceptual framework in this respect is informed by four key feminist theoretical insights:

i. Sexuality, like gender, is a social construction. The diversity of emotional and sexual expression across time and space flies in the face of beliefs that take sexuality as some innate natural expression (see Faderman 1985, Ortner and Whitehead 1981, Rubin 1975).

ii. There is a powerful relationship between gender and sexuality in contemporary Western societies. For example, the categories lesbian and heterosexual are dependent on the social production of gender difference (Butler 1990, Connell 1987, Rubin 1975). I argue that cultural understandings of sexuality will influence what we can achieve and how we experience ourselves as women and men, as well as how we relate across gender boundaries.

iii. That heterosexuality is a social institution that is central to the reproduction of patriarchy (Rich 1984). Its significance in supporting the status quo by providing the logic that draws men and women into relations of inequality gives it an institutional quality. This insight enables us to move beyond the more divisive focus on individual practice to one that is a more critical of social and ideological processes which police the boundaries of heterosexuality.

iv. The critique of the separate nature of the public and private spheres (Pateman 1988). This, for example, illuminates the relationship between the organization of homelife and paid work opportunities.

Although each of these insights has informed feminist research, I believe that I have been the first to recognize the advantage to be gained by combining all four together in empirically grounded research. Thus, a new series of questions are opened which are best explored though the lives of lesbian women. With such a sample we can ask, what is the nature of the social processes that enable them to be different and, importantly, what difference does this difference make?

I began to explore these questions in my book *Lesbian Lifestyles: Women's Work and the Politics of Sexuality.* This was based on a life-history study of continuity and change in the lives of 60 non-heterosexual British women aged 17 to 60. In interviews, the women were encouraged to speak of their journey through heterosexuality, possibly marriage, and beyond. Woven into this were their remembrances of childhood, of schooling (see also Dunne, 1992), information about their employment and domestic lives. Within all the complexity of respondents' autobiographies, commonalities could be identified–one of the most striking being the relationship between lesbianism and empowerment. It could be seen, for example, that a lesbian lifestyle both *necessitates* and *facilitates* financial self-reliance. In contrast to heterosexual experience, respondents described their lesbian relationships as based on notions of co-independence. Thus, the capacity to make primary relationships with women, rather than men, central *necessitates* long-term financial self-reliance. This knowledge informed the decisions of the many respondents who had returned to education or changed their occupations on 'coming out.' The link between lesbianism and the need to earn a living wage helps explain why lesbians are likely to hold higher qualifications and/or be in male-dominated occupations. Additionally, women's relationships with women were reported as *facilitating* their engagement with paid employment, through the support and encouragement they experienced from their partners and the more egalitarian domestic arrangements negotiated.

Lesbians may represent a different kind of worker for sociological analysis in so far as their relationship to employment opportunities is less distorted by gender processes than heterosexual women and men. For example, their approach to paid work is unlikely to be constrained by notions and practices that support the idea that women are secondary workers, nor are they likely to be inflated by those that support the notion that men should be providers. This was dramatically illustrated by their occupational diversity and the way that their pay (usually a living wage) fell roughly half way between the averages found for women and men more generally.

The implications of these findings for feminist thinking about work, and the relationship between gender and sexuality, are profound. They would suggest, for example, that women who have moved beyond the confines of heterosexuality engage with the 'public' and 'private' under far more favourable conditions than heterosexual women (Dunne 1997). Further, the relationship between the lesbian lifestyle and material empowerment seriously undermines notions of sexuality as an individual choice or 'private' issue. I would argue that as more women become educationally and financially empowered, lesbianism will become an increasingly common choice. Lesbian experience illuminates a complex relationship between sexuality and gender. For example, much of what has been conceptualized as simply gender constraints in the abstract are likely to relate to the heterosexual context which frames most women's gendered experience (see Dunne 1998b).

My current research takes up this issue of empowerment in lesbian women's domestic and market lives by exploring whether such factors hold for lesbian couples with dependent children. We know that in heterosexual partnerships the transition into parenthood heralds the emergence or entrenchment of inequality. Like their hetero-sexual peers, the negotiation of lesbian parenting in Britain takes place in an ideological and political context that treats childcare as a private responsibility. Paid work opportunities are structured around a 'masculine model of employment' (Bradley 1989) which fails to recognize that parents have responsibilities and time com-mitments beyond the formal workplace. Because divisions of labor in lesbian partnerships are negotiated by actors who occupy the same position in the gender hierarchy and share broadly similar gendered skills and experience, they present a marvelous opportu-nity to see what is achievable when gender polarization as a struc-turing principle is absent. Would the similarities lesbians share as women, and their positioning outside conventionality, enable the construction of more egalitarian approaches to parenting and the allocation of waged and unwaged work? If so, their experience may provide models for feminists, regardless of how they define their sexuality.

The findings from this study (based on 37 lesbian couples with dependent children) provide strong evidence to counter the logic behind the gendering of labor (see Dunne 1998a). Crucially the majority of the couples did achieve fairly balanced arrangements in relation to the allocation of waged and unwaged labor. Biological motherhood was a poor indicator of employment differences (hours, income, status) between partners. In contrast to evidence for heterosexual mothers, the parents in our sample were able to devote a far greater amount of time to childcare than domestic work. Their more child-centred time-use patterns were the logical outcome of an egalitarian approach to domestic work (the sharing of the domestic burden freed up their time) and the balancing of employment responsibilities in partnerships (so that neither partner had particu-larly long paid working hours). This outcome illuminates the irra-tionality and inefficiency of the gendered approaches that dominate heterosexual practice.

Our capacity as feminists to identify those factors which facili-tate and those which hinder the momentum of change in relation to the creation of fairer approaches to work and family life in partner-ships can be greatly enhanced by incorporating lesbian experience. In this, far more complex interactions between gender and sexuality, and the organization of paid and unpaid work are revealed than have previously been recognized. The flexibility that lesbians experience around who does what, for example, illuminates an important interconnection between sexuality and gender accountability. Household theorists, such as Berk (1985), explain the persistence of the gender segregation of household tasks, such as ironing and car maintenance, as linking the *musts* of work to be done with the *shoulds* of gender ideal. What gets ignored here is that this outcome is assured because heterosexuality is about the affirmation of difference (Butler 1990, Rubin 1975). If gender can be conceptualized as a process, something which individuals do and have done to them (Fenstermaker et al. 1991, Connell 1987), I argue, that there is an additional unacknowledged gender dimension to this process–that the gender of the person one is doing gender for/with makes a difference (Dunne 1998b).

Theorising gender inequalities in the labor market can also become more precise. It is commonly accepted that men's capacity to retain their employment advantage rests fairly heavily on their ability to appropriate the unwaged labor of women. Clearly for this to happen women and men must be or *anticipate being* in relationships with each other. The incorporation of research on divisions of labor between lesbian women shows that our investigation of the process of appropriation needs to get behind 'the family,' heterosexual co-habitation or marriage and recognize the significance of heterosexuality itself as both the logic and medium through which this appropriation occurs.

The 'solutions' found by most respondents to the contradiction between time to earn a living and time for children offer more general insights for feminist thinking on change. Their approaches, based on compromise and balance so that each partner leads a more integrated life, suggest that egalitarian outcomes are dependent on the re-framing of the boundaries of gender and the rethinking about what counts as valuable. The past 20 years have witnessed radical changes in what it means to be a woman; our direction needs now to be turned towards encouraging men to become more like women, and to undermining a masculine model of employment which places a higher value on market work over other important activities that have been associated with women. Further, contemporary debates on the 'crisis' of marriage and of the family may actually be missing what lies behind the dissatisfaction many women face in their relationships with men. My work suggests that this might not be simply a crisis of marriage but a crisis of heterosexuality itself. As the identities available to women increase, and alternatives for financing our existence in the world are found, there may be an ever-increasing conflict between women's expectations and the logic of gender difference that underpins heterosexuality.

The essays that follow provide powerful ammunition to counter the dominant image of lesbian experience as 'exotic' and 'other,' relevant only to debates about difference and sexuality. They illustrate both the commonalities lesbians share with other women and the significance of their more specific experience for informing wider feminist debates on work and family life.

REFERENCES

Berk, S. F. (1985) *The Gender Factory: The Apportionment of Work in American Households*, New York: Plenum.

Bradley, H. (1989) *Men's Work, Women's Work*, Cambridge: Polity.

Butler, J. (1990) *Gender Trouble: Feminism and the Subversion of Identity*, London: Routledge.

Connell, R. W. (1987) *Gender and Power*, Cambridge: Polity.

Dunne, G. A. (1992) 'Differences at Work: Perceptions of Work from a Non-Heterosexual Point of View' in H. Hinds and J. Stacey (eds) *New Directions in Women's Studies in the 1990s*, London: Falmer Press.

Dunne, G. A. (1997) *Lesbian Lifestyles: Women's Work and the Politics of Sexuality*, London: MacMillan and Toronto: University of Toronto Press.

Dunne, G. A. (1998a) 'Pioneers Behind Our Own Front Doors': Towards New Models in the Organization of Work in Partnerships' *Work Employment and Society* (June 1998).

Dunne, G. A. (1998b) 'A Passion for 'Sameness'?: Sexuality and Gender Accountability' in E. Silva and C. Smart (eds) *The 'New' Family?* London: Sage.

Faderman, L. (1985) *Surpassing the Love of Men: Romantic Friendship and Love Between Women from the Renaissance to the Present*, London: The Women's Press.

Fenstermaker, S., West, C., Zimmerman, D. H. (1991) 'Gender Inequality: New Conceptual Terrain' in Blumberg, R. L. (ed) *Gender, Family and Economy, The Triple Overlap*, London: Sage.

Ortner, S., B. and Whitehead, H. (eds) (1981) *Sexual Meanings: The Cultural Construction of Gender and Sexuality*, Cambridge: Cambridge University Press.

Pateman, C. (1988) *The Sexual Contract*, Cambridge: Polity Press.

Rich, A. (1984) 'On Compulsory heterosexuality and Lesbian Existence' in Snitow, A., Stansell, C., and Thompson, S. (eds) *Desire: The Politics of Sexuality*, London: Virago.

Rubin, G. (1975) The Traffic in Women: Notes on the "Political Economy" of Sex, in R.R. Reiter (ed.) *Towards an Anthropology of Women*, London: Monthly Review Press.

Making a Mockery of Family Life?
Lesbian Mothers in the British Media

Pam Alldred

SUMMARY. In Britain, the legal treatment of lesbian mothers and co-parents has improved considerably over the past 15 years (Harne et al., 1997). Despite this, they are still vilified in occasional outbursts in the popular press. This article identifies arguments against lesbian parenting employed in a recent front-page 'fury' article in a British daily tabloid newspaper, *The Sun*. Encouragingly, of the five arguments about the 'dangers' of lesbian parenting that can be identified in earlier legal battles (such as the 'risk' that children grow up gay, or become 'gender confused'), the only one which this article manages to present very convincingly is that of social stigma. Concern that the children of lesbians may experience name-calling or exclusion is, of course, a problem of discrimination and not a prob-

Pam Alldred's PhD is about the value of identity politics and of 'post-identity' thinking in current political debates about parents and children, and about lone mothers and lesbian mothers in particular. After a first degree in psychology, she has studied cultural studies and sociology and taught psychosocial and women's studies. She was part of the *Challenging Women: Psychology's Exclusions, Feminist Possibilities* (Buckinghamshire: Open University Press, 1996) and *Psychology, Discourse, Practice* (London: Taylor and Francis, 1996) book collectives. Outside of academic work she is involved in feminist campaigns on family law issues and anarcho/eco/feminist activism. Her current research work is about children's perspectives on home-school relations.

Address correspondence to Pam Alldred, Social Sciences Research Centre, South Bank University, 103 Borough Road, London SE1 0AA, UK.

[Haworth co-indexing entry note]: "Making a Mockery of Family Life? Lesbian Mothers in the British Media." Alldred, Pam. Co-published simultaneously in *Journal of Lesbian Studies* (The Haworth Press, Inc.) Vol. 2, No. 4, 1998, pp. 9-21; and: *Living "Difference": Lesbian Perspectives on Work and Family Life* (ed: Gillian A. Dunne) The Haworth Press, Inc., 1998, pp. 9-21; and: *Living "Difference": Lesbian Perspectives on Work and Family Life* (ed: Gillian A. Dunne) Harrington Park Press, an imprint of The Haworth Press, Inc., 1998, pp. 9-21. Single or multiple copies of this article are available for a fee from The Haworth Document Delivery Service [1-800-342-9678, 9:00 a.m. - 5:00 p.m. (EST). E-mail address: getinfo@haworthpressinc.com].

9

lem that is intrinsic to lesbian parenting (in contrast, say, to an argument about 'the psychology of lesbianism'). The rhetorical force of the piece comes from easily deconstructed journalistic techniques rather than coherent arguments. The sharpest condemnation of these women is actually for having a child whilst on welfare benefits. It is, therefore, economic concerns about 'state dependency,' rather than sexuality *per se*, which fuel the attack. The imagined financial self-sufficiency of heterosexual families which underpins this argument is outdated in its presumption of a bread-winning, male head of household. The fact that two days before the UK's 1997 General Election, the birth of a baby to a lesbian couple was granted front-page coverage is a sobering reminder of the hostility that lesbians still face through the scrutiny of their 'fitness to parent' and the intrusive condemnation of non-heterosexual domestic arrangements and relationships. *[Article copies available for a fee from The Haworth Document Delivery Service: 1-800-342-9678. E-mail address: getinfo@haworthpressinc.com]*

This is how the new British book *Valued Families: The Lesbian Mothers' Legal Handbook* (Harne and Rights of Women, 1997) begins:

> There are now far more lesbians openly raising children than at any time in the past. More lesbians are choosing to have children through donor insemination, and the opportunity for lesbians to foster or adopt children has become a reality. Coming out as a lesbian no longer means that the courts automatically regard a mother as unsuitable to bring up her children, and lesbian co-parents can now receive legal recognition of their parenting role. (p. xi)

This advice book updates the 1986 edition and shows how much things have changed in Britain over the past ten to fifteen years, from the idea that lesbian mothers were deviant, sexually irresponsible women whose children would grow up 'scarred,' might be 'in danger,' and were 'at risk of growing up gay' (Harne et al., 1997). It testifies to the progress that has been made as a result of feminist campaign work, and the broader shifts in gender relations and sexual relationships in Western cultures. The book asserts with confidence and the support of research findings, that 'being brought up by lesbian parents can be positively beneficial for children' (p. xi). Indeed, some of the researchers whose work has been invaluable for legal practitioners in the UK, such as Fiona Tasker and Susan Golombok, are contributors to this volume. Research on the 'outcomes' for children growing up in US lesbian households has been available for longer and is often of larger samples, but courts in the UK do value British studies.

However, despite this good news in the legal sphere, the institution of heterosexuality remains the privileged site of romantic and sexual investments, and the heterosexual nuclear family the privileged site for childrearing. The power of these normative ideas is such that other forms of sexual and familial relationships are belittled, denied and condemned (Barrett and McIntosh, 1982). The British media manifests fury and condemnation in its sporadic outbursts against lesbian mothers and other women whose fitness to mother is deemed questionable (see, for instance, Alldred, 1996). A recent newspaper article in a British daily paper, *The Sun*, reported 'fury' at the birth of a baby through self-insemination to a lesbian couple. *The Sun* is Britain's largest circulation national daily newspaper. It is one of the tabloids (as opposed to the 'quality' broadsheets) and is part of Rupert Murdoch's News International conglomerate. The arguments against lesbian parenting were not unique to this piece, indeed they draw on themes which are common throughout Western culture. Such meanings form the context in which lesbians live and love, and into which we publish research, even when some specific academic contexts are less hostile. The article is examined thematically, and is viewed as a cultural object which must be firmly located in the particular political and cultural context of its publication (including some of the articles that surround it, as well as the date and 'moment' of its publication). Its tone contrasts with the increasing legal recognition and respect shown to lesbian mothers and co-parents. However, it is understood as both reflecting and reinforcing certain negative cultural discourses of lesbianism, of motherhood and of welfare 'dependency.'

Some of the arguments against lesbian mothering that used to be heard in court–and the offensive questioning of a woman about her sexual practice–might now seem laughable had they not caused such pain to individual women. However, these arguments can still be alluded to, even where they would not be stated explicitly and so can still do damage. This newspaper article is interesting for the disjunction between the passionate language of 'fury' and the paucity of actual objections raised, and the prominence of the piece is remarkable given the events occurring in British politics at the time.

FRONT PAGE FURY

The headline *'Lesbians Pay £5 for a Baby'* dominated the front page of *The Sun* on Tuesday, April 29th, 1997. The article was continued on page 4, where it occupied nearly the whole page, and included statements from the women concerned, as well as comment from public figures and the newspaper's resident agony aunt. A third of the editorial on page 6 was devoted to the issue (and the rest was about Tony Blair). Under the heading *'Family Values,'* it declared that: *'Lesbians advertising for sperm degrade the act of procreation.'* It is ironic that a paper which is infamous for its soft-porn photographs of topless women can simultaneously be so sanctimonious about procreative heterosex. The readers' telephone poll that day also took up this issue, asking readers 'Should lesbians have children?' (The following day's paper claimed that: *'Sun Readers Want Lesbian Mums Ban,'* although no figures were given.)

In the days before the British General Election of 1st May, 1997, there were confident whispers of a landslide victory for the 'Left of centre' Labour Party, and that the Blairs would replace the Majors as the occupants of 10 Downing Street. In general, British national newspapers have quite blatant political party allegiances which tend to persist over time. However, on the day after the election campaign was declared in March came: *'An historic announcement from Britain's number 1 newspaper: THE SUN BACKS BLAIR: Give change a chance.'* *The Sun* had switched allegiance from the Conservative (or Tory) Party, the Government in power under John Major, to the Labour Party under Tony Blair's leadership as *'New* Labour.' The paper swung its full weight behind Blair as the Election Eve edition headline shows: *'Who Blair's Wins: Britain's Crying Out for Him.'* It is remarkable, therefore, that two days before an election, at a time of national news abundance and of the paper's own new and passionate editorial message, the issue of lesbian parenting was deemed fit for front-page fury. It is also significant that an article of this tone still has a place after this supposed 'ideological' shift to the Left, which is something I will return to later.

Underneath the main headline, the sub-header is '*Fury at DIY pregnancy.*' In the British context, DIY stands for 'do it yourself.' For some years it has referred to home improvements, but more recently it has been used to describe community activism that eschews conventional politics and services. In each case, 'doing it yourself' is in contrast or preference to having professionals do it for you. Here it constructs a lesbian woman's pregnancy by self-in-semination as amateurish. It implies that the conception is improper because it's outside of institutional or male control (Radford, 1991). As the agony aunt, Deirdre, notes, had they had enough money to pay a private clinic (the National Health Service had refused Rachel because of her sexuality) we might never have heard of them. Although they may have been saved this public scrutiny, their desire to parent would have been subjected to the intense profes-sional scrutiny reserved for those who fall outside the 'normal' category of women for whom motherhood is still seen as 'natural' (Marshall, 1991; Morell, 1994). Requesting reproductive services brings a medical gaze upon both desire and 'fitness to parent' that fertile heterosexual couples seldom have to face (Alldred, 1996; Woollett, 1991).

Exactly whose 'fury' the headline refers to remains unspecified. However, even unattributed, the word gives the article its tone. As often occurs in tabloid journalism, the headline promises heights of scandal which the article fails to deliver. Readers' interest is caught and their appetites whet, but many *Sun* readers must laugh at and mock the often exaggerated, salacious and corny headlines. Other journalistic techniques are employed to undermine the status of this (self-identified) lesbian 'family.' I will describe the explicit argu-ments made against lesbian parenting together with some of the implicit ways in which negative associations are made and more extreme arguments alluded to, through the framing of the article and the phrasing of the points.

BUYING BABIES?

As the article unfolds, we learn that the '£5 for a baby' was, in actual fact, £5 paid for an advert through which a lesbian couple recruited a donor. However, moral outrage is conjured by making it sound as if they bought a baby. It is intriguing that this moral tone can be maintained once it is revealed that their crime was not buying, marketing or eating babies, but hoping to raise one lovingly! The front page photograph is of two smiling women; the one in the foreground beams proudly as she holds a baby girl in a checked dress. It seems a happy, relaxed, *posed for* picture, a genuine 'family snap,' rather than an intrusive snapshot to which they did not consent. Either they gave the journalist this picture, along with the one of heavily pregnant Rachel standing face-to-face with Ellen, or allowed the *Sun* photographer in, believing that the article would be sympathetic. The strongest grounds for claiming the article to be an 'Exclusive' are that these lesbians trusted a tabloid journalist to interview them. Of course, the layout (as it exists) and the selection of headlines and quotations would have been the work of the sub-editor, not the journalist.

The article begins: 'A JOBLESS lesbian couple sparked fury last night. . . .' Having 'jobless' in capitals sets up a line of criticism over their employment status that is continued a few sentences later: 'The lesbians pick up £200 a week in state benefits–and four-month-old Chloe's father will contribute nothing.' Of course, the mother of a small child might find herself equally criticised for going out to work, but here the real concern appears to be about 'tax-payers' money' being spent on welfare benefits. They are referred to as 'state benefits,' rather than more sympathetic names like 'social security' or 'welfare benefits,' and referring to 'the lesbians' puts distance between them and the 'families' that might be seen as deserving of the Family Credit benefit. The prominence of this line of attack is significant given the weakness of the arguments made against lesbian parenting later in the piece.

Such hostility to people on benefits when they are constructed as undeserving or as 'underclass' might have been expected of the old (Conservative-allied) *Sun*, but to have this from the '*New Sun*' (supporting New Labour) can be viewed as an indication of shrinking ideological difference between the British political parties. It illustrates New Labour's 'tough line' on social issues, such as the 'Welfare to Work' proposals. Labour's shift away from socialist principles has introduced into the vocabulary the sarcastic use of the word 'New' to suggest policy U-turns or false continuities. With an increasing separation of politics from ideology, it becomes easier to see how a newspaper could switch between the two main parties.

The article's second sentence is: 'Crop-haired Rachel Henshaw, 24, gave birth to daughter Chloe after a gay Brazilian student answered their plea.' In a sentence with a lot of information to convey, 'crop-haired' is accorded significance (and this description of the father quietly activates hostility against some of *The Sun*'s regular targets). Whilst cropped hair may be mainstream fashion for women (and men) in contemporary British culture, there remain some associations of dyke or butch. This implicitly mobilises a discourse of 'unfeminine,' contrasting it with 'true femininity' with which nurturant motherhood is associated. It can be seen as a veiled undermining of her fitness to parent either through ideas of 'proper women,' or associations that the 'respectable working-class' readership may have of crop-haired with 'thugs' or 'yobs' (which, in Britain, signifies unruly, working class young men) and, perhaps, the underclass. (A headline on page 2 positions New Labour and the readership in relation to 'yobs': ' "Horrified" Blair declares war on yobs.')

THE STATUS ACCORDED LESBIAN RELATIONSHIPS

Rachel and Ellen live together with Ellen's five-year-old daughter. Rachel is quoted saying: '. . . We're a perfect family,' and Ellen: 'My little daughter sometimes asks if Rachel is her daddy. She says she loves her. We try to explain she is mummy's partner. As the girls grow older, of course we will tell them everything.' Rachel even describes herself as having 'desperately wanted a baby' and having 'maternal instincts.' However, despite indicating that they embrace discourses of romantic love; of parental love for their child; of planning a child together; and of themselves as a family, the article itself never describes them as a family. They are 'the lovers,' not 'partners.' This is a sexualized, but not domesticated relationship. It sounds passionate (so at least challenges the image of lesbian sex as 'handholding'), but transient, and so less stable and committed than 'partners' and less permanent than a family. Implying that the relationship is based on passion and sexual love can reinforce the idea of selfish people driven by their desires. Indeed, the agony aunt declares that they '*have put their longing to be mums before Chloe's need to grow up in what feels to her and would be accepted by her peers as a normal home.*' This leaves unquestioned the desires of heterosexual people to have children and assumes for them a moral high-ground of less selfish reasons. Fanshawe (1996), for one, criticises the juxtaposition of homosexuals to 'family values' in recent popular rhetoric, and indeed, the newspaper article's wording (e.g., 'the lesbians') foregrounds the differences between this 'family' and 'the family' which is presumed to be heterosexual and biologically fertile (Van Every, 1991).

The other front-page visual claim on our attention is a picture of two of The Spice Girls, the all-girl band who've taken the British pop scene by storm. They are wearing nurses' uniforms and have their skirts hitched up and their bare legs interlocked. There is clearly a homoerotic undertone–as with much of their publicity–and the center-page spread on the 'doctors-and-nurses' theme promises that in tomorrow's edition they are 'in bed together!' It is assumed that *The Spice Girls'* public playfulness about lesbian sexuality will not offend *Sun* readers, but the commitment of two women to each other and their child will. This presents lesbianism as acceptable as a form of titillation for, and for consumption by, the presumed heterosexual readership, but not as a form of actual relationship. It admits the existence of lesbian desire, but sees it as girlish frolicking which will either be outgrown, or curbed by the institutions of heterosexuality, family and marriage. It undermines these women's relationship by constructing lesbian relationships as immature and retaining a privileged position for heterosexuality as the 'real thing.'

THE DANGERS ATTRIBUTED LESBIAN MOTHERING

Once again, vagueness about the sources of comments, such as 'The arrangement was branded an "absolute disgrace" by politicians and child-support groups,' allows strong statements to have an impact whilst only being attributed to unnamed people and ambiguously named organisations. However, the article ends with

statements from public figures who are positioned as moral commentators.

'Moral crusader' Victoria Gillick finds it grotesque that 'Two
women have rejected men, but want a man's baby,' and a Church of
England Minister suggests that the child be adopted because 'Lesbianism is immoral.' A Conservative Member of Parliament asks
'Who is going to pay to bring up this child?' adding that 'a child
needs a father not two mothers.' A Conservative ex-Minister of
Health describes the women as 'looking after their own self-inter-
ests and ignoring the child's problems.' Even the relatively liberal
agony aunt, Deirdre, reiterates the accusation of selfishness. She
says she understands that gay people can long to be parents too, but
'To choose to have a baby with no means to support it and when
you know the child may face prejudice and bullying is immature
and selfish.' Selfishness is an enduring theme in criticisms of mothers and remains powerful because it is constructed as antithetical to
true, virtuous motherhood (see also Alldred, 1996). This is the
article's strongest attack on these women's fitness to parent. The
idea that women 'let their hormones rule their heads' is complicit
with the discourse of women as driven by passion, not reason, and
hence in need of surveillance. It constructs these women as immature and, as lesbians, at risk of being either too feminine, or not
feminine enough!

The criticisms of these women can be compared with concerns
about lesbian parenting that have been raised in court (from Harne
et al., 1997; Saffron, 1996 and Woodcraft, 1997). Five issues identified can be summarised as: gender identity, gender role behavior
conformity, homosexuality, abuse and social stigma. A British
judge in a 1992 case, called a psychiatrist to respond to the following three issues of potential concern (from Woodcraft, 1997):
firstly, that the child might be involved in sexual activity in the
home–to which the psychiatrist emphasized that pedophilia has no
link with homosexuality and that most sexual abuse of children is
committed by heterosexual men; secondly, that the child would
grow up gay–for which there is no evidence (see for example
Tasker and Golombok, 1995); and thirdly, that the children would
be subjected to taunts and teasing. Neither of the first two 'arguments' are raised in this newspaper article, so perhaps feminists'

contestation of these associations and empirical research has had some impact here. Deirdre is convinced the child will face 'prejudice and bullying' and, presumably, social stigma is what is meant by 'the child's problems.' Children face discrimination on a range of issues, and bullying is often about weight or social skills, and is certainly not particular to family form. In the case described by Woodcraft (1997), the expert argued that the child would be better equipped to deal with any taunts if she lived with women who felt positive about being lesbians, rather than with a heterosexual father's new family who were homophobic. The issue of social stigma is of real concern, but, as Harne et al. (1997) note, for courts to assume it, can reinforce such prejudice. The two remaining issues concern children's psychosexual development. Children's 'gender identity' refers to their sense of themselves as male or female, and 'gender-role behavior' to their conformity to gender stereotypes. These two, along with whether children 'grow up gay,' are psychological concerns, and the 'children need a father' argument–presented in this article–could be seen as a weak attempt to mobilize these, but in this context appears to be about fathers as providers. Tasker and Golombok's (1995) research provides evidence for responding reassuringly to these concerns and we may also want to challenge normative ideas about what boys and girls should be. These psychological arguments would present a more powerful case against lesbian parenting, but are not effectively deployed in this piece.

Thus, the most forceful arguments against lesbian parenting in the article are about social stigma and financial provision for the child. For instance, Deirdre does not present arguments about the nature of lesbian parenting itself, that is, problems intrinsic to the lesbian parent-child relationship, such as about the mental health or psychological qualities of lesbians. Instead, her main points are both social, rather than psychological. Stigma is a social problem of discrimination, and the child's financial support is one of economics and social welfare. Economics, or what it seen as 'tax-payers' money,' is a core concern underlying this fury about these women having a child. It is not their sexuality, but their receipt of benefits that fuels the condemnation.

CORRUPTION: NEW LABOUR AND OLD PREJUDICES

For a newspaper newly embracing the Labour Party there is an interesting preponderance of Conservatives amongst the moral commentators. Earlier concerns about children and gay men spoke of the risk of 'corruption.' This has faded, or is, at least, not voiced explicitly. Of concern today to those on the Left, is the corruption of the Labour Party's ideas about welfare and social issues by right-wing discourses of 'morality.' The fact that *The Sun's* party political allegiance can swing from Conservative to Labour whilst key ideo-logical areas such as 'family values' stay the same suggests internal contradictions either within the paper's perspective or within New Labour's position. Perhaps both. Any newspaper will contain a range of discourses on any given topic and there is no reason to assume consensus amongst staff at *The Sun,* and New Labour's commitments to progressive social reform and equalities issues are of concern to many on the Left in Britain. More broadly, the idea that the Left/Right ideological distinctions of Western politics are collapsing, is relevant here too.

Are these women making a 'mockery of family life' as the edito-rial claims? Lesbian mothering can only be understood as 'a mock-ery of family life' where family life is understood as being defined by the financial dependence of women and children on men. Judges, now used to seeing lesbian mothers, increasingly treat them as mothers first and lesbians second (Woodcraft, 1997), and attacks on lesbian mothers are mostly the same as those on mothers (and women) in general (Harne et al., 1997). The particularly harsh treatment of lone mothers in both the UK and US condemns women for having families independently of men.

The themes identified in this particular newspaper article are not uncommon amongst representations of lesbian relationships and mothering in Anglo-American dominated cultures. They are reminders that heterosexuality and the family remain powerful social institutions despite many sites of liberalization (including some aspects of the legal sphere), and because they are presented as *the* sites of romantic and nurturant love, alternative forms of sexual and parental relations are undermined. Because the nuclear family claims romantic and nurturant love for itself, alternatives become harder to forge and sustain since they receive less social recognition and because ritual and expression are limited (McIntosh, 1996).

The criticisms that lesbians face and their hostility towards their relationships and domestic arrangements should not be presented (or responded to) as 'lesbian problems' or problems of lesbianism. They are, rather, part of the cultural problem of a lack of tolerance of difference and of conservative moral authoritarianism. To locate the problem with lesbian women, or welfare recipients, or to construct social stigma as 'this child's problem' is to blame the 'victim' (of stigma, intolerance) and to scapegoat those who bear difference. Right-wing discourses of 'family values' link heterosexuality, family form, and parenting in ways that are essentialist. They not only obscure, but pathologize alternatives. Such is the sometimes hostile cultural setting for women who are living difference. It is also, of course, the context in which our research about lesbian lives may be heard. We must ensure that our empirical work, and the way we present it, cannot implicitly reinforce these themes. The following chapters in this volume identify some of the ways in which the institution of heterosexuality impacts on the lives of lesbians in particular national and cultural contexts. They also demonstrate moments and ways in which women resist such pressures. By examining the normative presumptions within discourses of 'the family,' we may be better placed to articulate criticisms, and by exploring through empirical research the precise forms taken by discourses of 'the family' in the lives of particular women, we may be better able to recognize and support the alternative sites of nurturant and romantic love.

REFERENCES

Alldred, Pam (1996) "'Fit to parent'? Developmental psychology and 'non-traditional' families" in E. Burman, P. Alldred, C. Bewley, B. Goldberg, C. Heenan, D. Marks, J. Marshall, K. Taylor, R. Ullah and S. Warner *Challenging Women: Psychology's Exclusions, Feminist Possibilities*, Buckinghamshire, Open University Press. pp 141-159.

Barrett, Michele and McIntosh, Mary (1982) *The Anti-Social Family*, London: Verso.

Fanshawe, Simon (1996) 'One for all and all for mum,' *The Pink Paper* (25th October, 1996).

Harne, Lynne and Rights of Women (1997) *Valued Families: The Lesbian Mothers' Legal Handbook*, London: The Women's Press.

McIntosh, Mary (1996) 'Social anxieties about lone motherhood and ideologies of the family: two sides of the same coin,' in Silva E. B. (ed.) *Good Enough Mothering: Feminist Perspectives on Lone Motherhood*, London: Routledge. pp 148-156.

Marshall, Harriette (1991) 'The social construction of motherhood: an analysis of child-care and parenting manuals,' in A. Phoenix, A. Woollett and E. Lloyd (eds) *Motherhood: Meanings, Practices and Ideologies*, London: Sage. pp 66-85.

Morell, Carolyn (1994) *Unwomanly Conduct: The Challenges of Intentional Childlessness*, New York: Routledge.

Radford, Jill (1991) 'Immaculate Conceptions,' *Trouble and Strife*, 21 (Summer): 8-12.

Saffron, Lisa (1996) *'What about the children?' Sons and Daughters of Lesbian and Gay Parents Talk About Their Lives*, London: Cassell.

Tasker, Fiona and Golombok, Susan (1995) 'Adults Raised as Children in Lesbian Families,' *American Journal of Orthopsychiatry*, 65: 203-215.

Van Every, Jo (1991) 'Who is 'the family'? The assumptions of British social policy,' *Critical Social Policy*, 33 (Winter 1991/1992): 62-76.

Woodcraft, Elizabeth (1997) 'Lesbian parents–changing attitudes,' *Rights of Women Bulletin*, (Rights of Women, London, UK) (Summer 1997): 27-30.

Woollett, Anne (1991) 'Having Children: Accounts of Childless Women and Women with Reproductive Problems,' in A. Phoenix, A. Woollett and E. Lloyd (eds) *Motherhood: Meanings, Practices and Ideologies*, London: Sage. pp 47-65.

Getting Kids and Keeping Them: Lesbian Motherhood in Europe

Kate Griffin

SUMMARY. This article looks at two major issues faced by lesbian mothers in Europe: getting kids and keeping them. The first part focuses on the ways lesbians have children, and in particular the different levels of access to formal insemination services for lesbians in European countries. The second part examines custody issues faced by lesbians with children from previous heterosexual relationships, and those faced by lesbians who have children within a lesbian relationship; and legal recognition of the bond between non-biological parents and their children. The article is based on original research and interviews carried out by the author for the book *Lesbian Motherhood in Europe*. *[Article copies available for a fee from The Haworth Document Delivery Service: 1-800-342-9678. E-mail address: getinfo@ haworthpressinc.com]*

Kate Griffin has been living in Moscow with her partner since 1995, where she has worked for a variety of Russian and British news organizations. From 1991-1995 she worked as a project manager for Brussels-based CREW (Centre for Research on European Women), specialising in partnerships with women's organizations in central and eastern Europe and Russia. From 1989-1991 she worked for a reference publishing company in Cambridge. From 1985-1989 she read modern languages at Cambridge University. She has published various articles on lesbian motherhood, and is co-editor, with Lisa A. Mulholland, of *Lesbian Motherhood in Europe*, Cassell, 1997. She has one daughter, Alba.

Address correspondence to Kate Griffin, Springfield, St. George's Avenue, King's Stanley, Stonehouse, Glos GL10 3HN, UK (e-mail: kgriffin@glasnet.ru).

[Haworth co-indexing entry note]: "Getting Kids and Keeping Them: Lesbian Motherhood in Europe." Griffin, Kate. Co-published simultaneously in *Journal of Lesbian Studies* (The Haworth Press, Inc.) Vol. 2, No. 4, 1998, pp. 23-34; and: *Living "Difference": Lesbian Perspectives on Work and Family Life* (ed: Gillian A. Dunne) The Haworth Press, Inc., 1998, pp. 23-34; and: *Living "Difference": Lesbian Perspectives on Work and Family Life* (ed: Gillian A. Dunne) Harrington Park Press, an imprint of The Haworth Press, Inc., 1998, pp. 23-34. Single or multiple copies of this article are available for a fee from The Haworth Document Delivery Service [1-800-342-9678, 9:00 a.m. - 5:00 p.m. (EST). E-mail address: getinfo@haworthpressinc.com].

GETTING KIDS

Lena from Russia has always known herself to be a lesbian, but since she was a child she knew she would definitely have children. 'I entered into sexual relations with men only with that goal,' she said wryly.

At the beginning of the 1980s it was unusual for lesbians in the Netherlands to think of having kids, according to Moniek, but she was coming up to her 30th birthday and felt the biological clock ticking away. Her girlfriend thought it would be fun, as long as she didn't have to be pregnant herself. Moniek asked an old friend with whom she had had a relationship years ago to father the child. After thinking it over for a few months he agreed, but didn't want to take on the role of father, because he spent a lot of time travelling.

'The first time I did it by making love with him but we were laughing all the time,' Moniek explained with a smile. 'Then I realized that when you do this for several months, it becomes weird. To do it once it's not a problem, but when you have to keep doing it to make a child it won't work out. Besides, my partner was having problems with it. So the second time he went to another room and knocked on the door five minutes later saying, "here you have what you need."' Moniek's girlfriend took the semen and did the insemination, and Moniek became pregnant.

Their son Koen has always known the facts of his conception, and at primary school he would quite happily explain his family set-up to his friends. At first they accepted that he had two mothers without question, but once they started to learn the facts surrounding conception they began to ask how it was possible. So Koen would tell them. 'You know of course I have a father. But my mothers love each other so they live together and my father, well, he is a friend, and you need that for the seed.'

Kati from Finland became a mother when she got involved with a woman with a four-year-old daughter. A few years later her lover had a son, with the help of a donor. Now the couple have separated, but Kati still sees her children regularly.

Clare and Debbie from the UK fell in love in 1983, when they were both twenty-two. Four years into their relationship, they decided it was time to have children. First Clare got pregnant and gave birth to John, then a few years later Debbie had Kevin. Both times they used sperm from donors who had no further involvement. The first in their circle of friends to have kids, they are still asked for advice by other lesbians wanting to become parents.

There is no set way in which lesbian mothers in Europe get their kids. The route they choose to parenthood depends on a mix of social and personal factors. Many lesbian mothers already have children when they come out as lesbians. Other lesbians find themselves with a ready-made family when they become involved with a woman with children. And in the last few years, many lesbians have decided to start a family with the help of donors or friends, regardless of the prevailing view in society that to be a lesbian mother is a contradiction in terms.

Motherhood is not seen as an ideal throughout the lesbian community, however. In certain lesbian circles in Austria, Belgium, France, Germany and Italy, for example, lesbian mothers are seen as "traitors" for having had contact with men, and for focusing inward on their own family rather than outward on the lesbian community. Similarly, suspicion of latent heterosexuality was reported as a problem for lesbian mothers in Greece. But in other countries, such as Russia, sexuality and reproduction are seen as two different and often unconnected aspects of a woman's life, and the desire to have children is not tied to expectations of marriage or of having a male partner. For Russian women, having children is what some women may choose to do at some point in their life, whereas having a husband may not be part of that choice. Many lesbians had children when they were young, either before or after they embraced their lesbianism. Just as motherhood is not divided into lesbian and non-lesbian, similarly many Russian lesbians do not divide themselves into mothers and non-mothers.

The two major issues currently facing lesbian and gay families across Europe are how to get children, and how to keep them. Access to insemination, custody, and legal recognition of the relationship between lesbian and gay parents and their children are subjects currently high on the agenda of lesbian and gay movements in many European countries.

Informal insemination is available to lesbians across Europe, as long as they can find willing donors. It is generally difficult for the state to intervene in such private arrangements. But ease of access to formal insemination services for lesbians and policies toward lesbian clients vary from country to country. Official insemination services are not available in Croatia, Hungary, Latvia or Slovakia. They are restricted to married couples in the Czech Republic, Germany, Greece, Italy, Lithuania and Sweden, but in Estonia, Slovenia and Spain single women have access to state insemination services. In Austria, Ireland and Serbia insemination services are available privately.

Insemination falls into a legal grey area and is not forbidden to lesbians in Norway, Poland and Russia. In Denmark, Finland and Switzerland it is up to the discretion of the doctor or hospital, while legislation in the UK states that the clinic should take into consideration the welfare of the child, including the need for a father.

There are some positive examples of clinics actively deciding not to discriminate against lesbians. Since 1981, a Brussels clinic has had as its official policy that there should be no discrimination of single women or lesbian couples in access to alternative insemination. The counsellor there reports that since she started work, she has seen fifty-two Belgian lesbian couples and about thirty French lesbian couples. Information about the clinic is circulated informally in France through gay circles. Many Dutch women over forty who have difficulty getting insemination in the Netherlands because of their age also travel to Brussels.

Another issue connected with alternative insemination for lesbians is the role of the donor. When insemination services and information about self-insemination started to become more widely available a few years back, many lesbians chose anonymous donors, generally to avoid having to fight for custody at a later date. Now the trend is toward asking male, often gay friends to be the donor, and establishing an amicable parenting arrangement right from the start.

A clinic in the Dutch town of Leiden offering insemination to lesbians has developed an approach to alternative insemination by a donor that holds the middle line between an anonymous donor and a known donor. The donor remains anonymous but is willing to deposit certain information about himself with a notary. The child, and only the child, can later retrieve this information, as well as the identity of the donor, if she or he wants to.

Right from the start, Clare and Debbie from the UK chose to be a two-parent family, without any contact with the donors. When their kids were born, especially the eldest, John, they felt the children were very precious and so were keen to keep them to themselves rather than share them with other adults, including the donors. "The children don't see themselves as having a father. That wasn't the relationship we entered into with the donors. To be fair to them, and more importantly to be fair to the kids, we've been quite clear about that from the start," explained Debbie. "The other thing to say" said Clare, "is that we're both mothers to both of them. Although biologically we've had one child each, they relate to us and we relate to them both as equal. They call us both mum–'Mum!' 'Yeah, what?' 'Not you, the other one.' "

KEEPING KIDS

A lesbian who became a mother during a previous heterosexual relationship may not have found it difficult to get her children, but keeping them once she has come out as a lesbian is another matter. Although the fear of losing children conceived during heterosexual relationships through custody battles is receding in some parts of Europe, lesbian mothers from many countries, including Austria, Bulgaria, Croatia, Czech Republic, Greece, Italy, Poland, Portugal, Russia and Serbia, would be reluctant to have their lesbianism disclosed in court for fear of losing the case and the children. Ex-husbands often use their knowledge of their former wife's lesbianism to exert pressure and get their own way. But in Portugal, one lesbian mother pointed out that courts do not always take seriously a husband's accusation of lesbianism against his wife, as the word "lesbian" is frequently used as an insult.

In the Czech Republic there is one known case of a lesbian mother going to court to fight for custody having cited her lesbianism as a reason for the divorce. She had to undergo a battery of psychological and other tests, but in the end she was awarded custody on the grounds that she and her new female partner were likely to be better parents for the ten-year-old boy than the remarried father and his new wife.

A lesbian mother from Italy told of a long and arduous two-year battle for the custody of her son, now ten, against a father who seemed to have everything on his side, including the Catholic church. His main advantage was that he knew of her lesbianism–and that she was living with her lover–which gave her little power to negotiate. Eventually she found a lawyer willing to act on her behalf, through the Italian lesbian and gay organisation Arci Gay Arci Lesbia, and managed to win almost equal custody rights. Although willing to be interviewed, even four years later she was adamant that her name should not appear in a book about lesbians for fear of possible repercussions.

The rights of the biological father are becoming more embedded in the legal structure of some countries in Europe, regardless of whether the biological father has also embraced the role of social father. In Germany, for example, there is a campaign to change the law regarding parental rights. Fathers want more rights over their children, and thus more control over the mothers, even when they live apart. In divorce and custody proceedings in Germany, an increasing number of judges do not take into account a mother's lesbianism. But the idea of shared custody has become popular with the youth welfare department and with judges. Shared custody concerns not the actual childcare, but the authority to make decisions like which school a child is going to attend. When a lesbian mother and her ex-husband are awarded shared custody, even if she becomes the primary caretaker, her former husband will have numerous ways to legally intervene in her future life.

Christina from eastern Germany found that ten years after their divorce, her ex-husband could still intrude into her life, despite having had virtually no contact with her or their son since then. Christina has full custody of her ten-year-old son, Philipp. Her only contact with her ex-husband has been through a children's rights agency, which ensures the continuation of the maintenance agreement. Her ex-husband has the right to visit the child, but has never exercised it. But when Christina and Philipp decided to change back to her maiden name, her ex-husband took offence and threatened to stop payments. 'At that moment, my biggest fear was of losing my child. I never told my ex-husband how I live–why should I? I saw him twice in the last five years. But now, dealing with the administration and writing official papers, I tried to hide what I am–a lesbian.'

Her main fear was that her ex-husband would suddenly decide to exert his right as the biological father to see the child, and prevent her from moving to another country to set up home with her lover. 'So in this case I wouldn't be able to move to Italy with my child, to live with my lover–lesbian lover!–because the biological father would say no.'

Christina is angry and frustrated by the unfairness of her situation: 'Is this the way? That a man–who never lived with the child, never really took care of him–can control my life for twenty or more years, although I divorced ten years ago and never met him again? It's such a serious danger for our lives, for our children, for ourselves.'

Fear of losing custody can prevent lesbian mothers from seeking any help, financial or otherwise, from the biological father of the child. In Poland every single parent has the right to receive maintenance, but Joanna does not plan to ask for any support from the biological father of her child, Justyna. Right from the start she set out to be an independent single parent, with little contact with the biological father after the conception. She took this decision knowing that attitudes in Poland are so hostile towards lesbian families that if she did ever decide to exert her right to ask for maintenance she would risk losing her child. If the biological father took her to court for custody and revealed that she is a lesbian, she would surely lose the case and probably evoke hostility to her and attempts to take the child. 'A number of Catholic families would appear and want to take my child so she could grow up in a good family with the right moral values. Not this family,' Joanna said, pointing to herself and Justyna.

Women in Poland have the right to a maternity allowance equivalent to a quarter of the average monthly salary. These payments are very small, so Joanna supplements her income by giving private lessons. Before Justyna was born, Joanna worked as a librarian, which is the lowest-paid profession in Poland: she is earning more while on maternity leave. During the three years of leave to which she is entitled, Joanna intends to look for another job.

Lesbian mothers in Russia can take advantage of a system that deliberately avoids attaching any stigma to single parenthood. The rules are such that a mother is under no obligation to name the father of her child, allowing lesbians to sidestep the possibility of later fights over custody. Lena, a single mother with three children, said she chose fathers who would not be interested in claiming custody. 'I never entered any father when I registered my children. This was part of a conscious policy.' In Russia, the mother or the father can take the documents from the hospital and register the birth of a child. The mother has to be indicated, but for the father there are three options: the spouse, a man who consents to be recognised as the father, or no father at all. By choosing the third option, Lena was able to ensure that she would be free from problems regarding custody, and that she would be officially recognised as a single mother.

As a single mother, Lena is entitled to state benefits, though nowadays they amount to very little. Money is a problem. Lena's monthly salary is the equivalent of 40 US dollars, so she has to take on additional work, leaving her little time to spend with her children.

Lena and her three children live in a tiny flat on the outskirts of Moscow. At weekends they are joined by Lena's girlfriend and her son. Freedom from the likelihood of custody battles does not make it any easier for Lena and her children to be open about their family set-up. The level of homophobia in Lena's home town is very high. 'The difficult part is making my relationship with my children as honest and open as I can without making them vulnerable to the aggressive heterosexual world,' Lena explains. 'The difficulty is in conveying the complexity of life: the world inside the home with the mother is one thing, the world outside is another.'

But Lena finds it hard to imagine life otherwise. 'Any ideas I might have for changing my life I do not make real because I would put my children in more danger than they already are,' she says. 'I cannot speak openly under my last name as a lesbian because I am afraid my children will be harassed. I can't open a business because I fear that in that case my children will be used to harass me–I would be vulnerable to racketeers[1] and put my children in danger of being kidnapped or killed. And I can't leave this country to go to a safer country because of my mother who is used to living here and wouldn't want to move. So I can only dream. . . . '

It is mostly lesbian mothers with children from former heterosexual relationships who fear custody battles and losing their kids.

Lesbians who decide to have children by self-insemination tend to have much more control over the agreement with the biological father, whether he is merely a donor or also the social father. In this case, the role of the biological father within the family is usually clearly spelled out in advance. Often the amount of time the biological father is to spend with the child, if at all, is decided before the child is born, leading to fewer arguments later. It is also agreed in advance what the biological father's financial contribution, if any, will be. If the biological father chooses to take on the role of social father as well, this is carefully negotiated beforehand, and he is welcomed into the family. Some lesbian mothers, especially with male children, have invited gay male friends to be part of the family, so that they can provide positive male role models for the children.

But family breakups also happen within lesbian families, and there are few sources of support and advice for lesbians with kids when they split up. The non-biological mother within the couple can find herself in a particularly difficult situation.

Kati from Finland has been through a lesbian family breakup and come out the other side, but although the relationship with her ex-lover is now on a fairly even keel, she often feels that her position as a separated lesbian co-mother is still rather precarious. Kati has a daughter of fourteen and a son of seven, both of whom visit her and her new lover regularly. Despite having been a full-time parent for six years before she and her lover separated, as a non-biological mother, Kati has no legal rights to her children at all. 'If I could do what I wanted, I would have the kids, at least the younger one, live at my place. But since there is nobody on my side, I must agree with whatever my former lover wants. Until now everything has gone well (we have been separated for four years), but every time there is a disagreement between us, she threatens me with the possibility of not seeing my kids any more.'

Kati has developed very strong feelings about the rights of non-biological mothers. She decries 'the myth of blood or flesh or genes in talking about kinship. Many lesbian bio-mothers also believe in this myth, and don't let their partners co-mother. Motherhood or parenthood is not in the blood or in the genes. Parenthood is social, not biological. Most parents just happen to be blood relatives to their children, but that doesn't say anything about their ability to parent. All adoptive and other non-biological parents can testify with me: when you learn to love a child, you can parent her or him just as the child's biological parent–or even better, because social parenthood is mostly chosen and voluntary. The secret of motherhood is in love, not in biology.'

Legal recognition of the bond between non-biological parents and their children is an issue that is particularly pertinent to lesbian and gay parents. In most European countries they are denied this recognition. The non-biological mother cannot adopt her children, as adoption rights are either limited to married couples, or single people are allowed to adopt only if the authorities believe them to be heterosexual. Even when both mothers want the non-biological mother to have legal rights and access to the child, the court rarely supports it.

When Moniek and her partner separated in 1993, after raising Koen together for the eleven years since his birth, they applied to an Amsterdam court to grant equal custody and visitation rights to the non-biological mother. 'We did this mostly because she was feeling insecure. She had helped raise him from the beginning. Since the separation, he spends half his time at her place down the block, the rest of the time with me. We feel she is still a parent.' Moniek felt they had a good chance of winning the case, as the custody law had been revised in 1985, making it possible for unmarried heterosexual couples to both have legal custody of their children.

The Amsterdam court ruled that, because the ex-partner had no legal parental relationship to the boy, she was not eligible for custody. Moniek explains: 'The law said that the other parent did not have to be the real parent, but that it had to be possible for that person to be the real parent.' In this case, real means biological, so that the person had to be a man. 'I said to the judge, you know, I can point out any man in the street and say ok, he can be the social parent [the term used for non-biological parent]. She's the social parent, she's taken care of him from before he was born until now, and it's weird to say that anyone else can be the parent but she cannot.' The judge showed some sympathy for her argument, according to Moniek, but still ruled against them. Moniek and her ex-partner then appealed against the verdict, arguing that the law regarding child custody would probably be revised further, and that they should both be allowed custody in anticipation of the change. They lost the appeal in June 1994.

Moniek and her ex-partner now have a good relationship, so access rights are not such an urgent issue. Despite their lack of success so far, they are determined to continue to fight the case in the future as a matter of honor, and to lead the way for other lesbian couples wanting equal custody rights.

Lobbying for legal acknowledgement of lesbian and gay relationships has been high on the agenda of lesbian and gay organisations in Europe for the last few years, with great success in some countries. At the time of writing lesbians can become registered partners in Denmark, Iceland, Norway and Sweden, and in the Netherlands from January 1998, while same-sex common law marriage is permitted in Hungary. But the legislation is not perfect, as it does not offer any protection to the relationship between partners and children to whom they are not biologically related. These laws confer the same legal rights and responsibilities as marriage, except for adoption and insemination rights.

Iceland is the only country with a law on registered partnerships which gives any rights to lesbian and gay couples regarding children. This law, which came into force on June 27, 1996 and is held up as a model of what can be achieved, gives lesbian and gay couples joint custody of the children of either partner. Both partners become the children's guardians and should the biological parent die, the non-biological parent automatically becomes their sole guardian. However, the law still does not permit adoption of children by gay or lesbian couples, nor does it provide for lesbians' right to artificial insemination.

So lesbians and gay men are exploring other avenues for legalizing the bond between non-biological parents and their children. Lesbians in the UK seeking equal rights for the non-biological mother have used the UK's Residency Order introduced by the 1989 Children's Act. This law allows a person who resides with a child to apply for parental rights over that child. Although the law was originally intended to give rights to, say, grandparents raising their grandchildren, it does not specify that the person applying for the residency order has to be biologically related to the child, simply that they should be a "significant adult" in the child's life. As well as giving parental rights to the non-biological mother, this residency order also provides a legal basis for agreeing access rights in the case of separation.

Clare and Debbie are one of the lesbian couples in the UK who have used this law successfully. 'The most exciting news is that Debbie and I are now LEGAL!' wrote Clare. 'Yes, we won our case and have been given shared parental rights for both the children. It's taken about a year and a half to go through the various court hearings and visits, and cost us a packet in the process.'

The high court costs are the main factor preventing many other lesbian couples from applying for a residency order. Clare and Debbie want to use their success to help other lesbian mothers gain the same rights. 'We've decided to have a party in a couple of months to celebrate and publicise our victory. It'll be a good excuse to have a knees up but also to support other women who want to do the same thing. We're thinking of setting up a fund for legal costs–we can just about afford to pay ours but it has cost us far more than we expected. When we started I was hardly earning anything and so could claim legal aid, but since I got my wages paid again we've had to foot all the bills ourselves.'

There is no doubt in Clare's and Debbie's minds that they did the right thing, despite the expense involved. 'It felt worth all of this just to hear the judge acknowledge that what we are doing is the best thing for the boys (not that we doubted it, but it felt important to have it recognised by the law). John and Kevin were delighted and wanted to tell everyone (including the milkman!). It's been very affirming for them–I think it will help them a lot in the next few years as they begin to encounter more hassle from their peers at school–at least they know that the highest court in the country has approved of and verified their lives as legitimate, so even if kids say they can't have two mums, they have a court order to prove otherwise.'

NOTE

1. Although the crime rate in Russia soared in 1993-4 and had begun to fall by the time of the interview in late 1995, awareness of crime was still high. Much crime focused on small business–anyone who started their own enterprise was particularly vulnerable to racketeers unless they had protection, which was often provided by other racketeers anyway.

Raising Children in an Age of Diversity–
Advantages of Having a Lesbian Mother

Lisa Saffron

SUMMARY. Research into the influence of parental lesbianism on child development has not revealed any meaningful nor significant differences between the children of lesbian and heterosexual parents. While such research helps to disprove negative assumptions about lesbian mothers, the focus has been on the potential problems and disadvantages of this difference from the norm. In interviews with 17 British teenagers and adults who have lesbian mothers, respondents suggested distinct advantages for themselves which they attributed to their mother's sexuality. They spoke of the influence their mothers had on their moral development, particularly on their awareness of prejudice and their acceptance of diversity and of homosexuality. They felt they had benefited from the insights they gained into gender relations and from the broader, more inclusive definition of family they acquired through growing up in a different kind of family. *[Article copies available for a fee from The Haworth Document Delivery Service: 1-800-342-9678. E-mail address: getinfo@haworthpressinc.com]*

Lisa Saffron is a health writer who has written books on lesbian parenting, including *What About the Children? Sons and Daughters of Lesbian and Gay Parents Talk About Their Lives* (Cassell, 1996) and *Challenging Conceptions–Planning a Family by Self-Insemination* (Cassell, 1994). She leads workshops for lesbians thinking about getting pregnant and gives information to anyone interested in the subject. She lives in Bristol with her partner and daughter.

Address correspondence to Lisa Saffron, 47 Seymour Road, Bishopston, Bristol BS7 9HS, England.

[Haworth co-indexing entry note]: "Raising Children in an Age of Diversity–Advantages of Having a Lesbian Mother." Saffron, Lisa. Co-published simultaneously in *Journal of Lesbian Studies* (The Haworth Press, Inc.) Vol. 2, No. 4, 1998, pp. 35-47; and: *Living "Difference": Lesbian Perspectives on Work and Family Life* (ed: Gillian A. Dunne) The Haworth Press, Inc., 1998, pp. 35-47; and: *Living "Difference": Lesbian Perspectives on Work and Family Life* (ed: Gillian A. Dunne) Harrington Park Press, an imprint of The Haworth Press, Inc., 1998, pp. 35-47. Single or multiple copies of this article are available for a fee from The Haworth Document Delivery Service [1-800-342-9678, 9:00 a.m. - 5:00 p.m. (EST). E-mail address: getinfo@haworthpressinc.com].

INTRODUCTION

When asked if she thought there were any advantages to having a lesbian mother, Katrina, the 17-year-old daughter of a lesbian-feminist mother, had no hesitation in replying,

> Having a lesbian mother has enabled me to have a head start on everybody else emotionally, psychologically, intellectually, in every way. I wouldn't know the things that I know, wouldn't be the person I am now, and I wouldn't be as assertive as I am now if I hadn't been brought up by a lesbian mother. My Mum has drilled it into me since I was small, that you stand up for yourself, you say what you want and you don't let any man tell you what to say or do.

This young woman was well aware of the negative attitudes towards lesbianism held by most of her peers and protected herself at school by not disclosing her mother's sexuality. Yet she readily attributed positive aspects of her upbringing to her mother's sexuality, reflecting a set of beliefs shared by members of many lesbian-led families. Without denying the impact of homophobic prejudice and ignorance, many lesbian mothers and their children perceive substantial benefits for children from growing up with lesbians who are open about their sexuality.

After many years of writing about lesbian motherhood from the mothers' perspective, I wanted to explore the experiences and perceptions of the offspring (Saffron 1996). Unlike their mothers, they are not consciously creating new kinds of families and positively asserting their identity. Their views could well be radically different from those of their mothers.

In 1995, I interviewed 17 people in Britain ranging in age from 11 to 66 years, all of whom had lesbian mothers. Respondents were recruited through lesbian contacts, by advertising in the national gay media, by sending leaflets to lesbian and gay centers in Britain and by asking lesbian mothers I knew of personally or was told about. The sample was not intended to be representative and is clearly biased towards people who have good relationships with their parents. The aim was for people with lesbian mothers to tell their stories in their own words, explaining the issues they had identified as important. Interviews were unstructured, with the focus on those aspects of their experience which relate in one way or another to having a lesbian parent.

Respondents were chosen to illustrate the diversity of people with lesbian mothers and the range of family structures created by lesbians. Yet, common themes emerged during the interviews, which indicate that the experience of having a lesbian mother can have positive advantages. These themes are in contrast to the narrow set of questions addressed by most of the research studies on children of lesbians. These questions are in response to the concerns of judges in custody cases, policy makers formulating rulings about adoption and fostering and psychologists interested in child development. Do the children develop normally? Are they confused about their gender identity? Do they behave in sex-stereotyped ways? Will they be lesbian or gay? Do they feel bad about themselves, have behavior problems or psychiatric disorders? Are they able to make friends with other children? Do they suffer from the stigma against homosexuality (see review articles by Golombok & Tasker 1997; Patterson 1992; 1995)? This body of research has not yet revealed any meaningful nor significant differences in psychological development between the children of lesbian and heterosexual parents.

According to the people I interviewed, there may well be meaningful differences in moral and social development. Respondents suggested that children raised by lesbian mothers have the potential to develop more accepting and broad-minded attitudes towards homosexuality, women's independence, the concept of family, and social diversity than children from families which conform more closely to the norm. The experience of having a lesbian mother gives children the advantage of learning by example, which is a more powerful teacher than explanation alone. Efforts by heterosexual parents to transmit progressive values to their children do not have the same relevance and immediacy since heterosexual parents are not modelling acceptance and pride in a stigmatised identity. Their unprejudiced views may remain theoretical or unexpressed, not deemed a suitable matter for discussion with young children or without an opportunity for demonstration. Four themes emerged from the interviews which are explored in more depth in this article.

ATTITUDES TOWARDS HOMOSEXUALITY

According to a recent British survey (Wellings et al., 1994), a distressingly large percentage of the British population, two-thirds of men and over half of women, say that they believe that homosexual sex is wrong. Prejudice towards homosexuality is a powerful force in society, impoverishing and damaging the lives of lesbians and gay men, many of whom will be prevented from fulfilling their full potential in life as a consequence. Lesbians and gay men are not the only ones to suffer from homophobia and the perpetrators of prejudice are as much its victims.

Prejudice leads to a distorted version of reality by rendering invisible as well as by misrepresenting the true experiences of lesbian and gay people. It leads to alienation by creating a category of 'other' from which heterosexual people dissociate themselves. It hinders people from exploring their own sexuality and understanding that sexuality is a continuum rather than fixed in two mutually exclusive categories. Prejudice is one of the motivations behind men's inability to form close bonds with each other, to participate fully in their children's upbringing, to step out of their masculine roles into that of a whole human being, and to relate to women on equal terms. Prejudice against homosexuality is one of the reasons heterosexual parents work so hard at enforcing culturally accepted notions of masculinity in their boy children and feminine characteristics in their girl children. Prejudice leads people to reject members of their families who disclose their homosexuality, including their own sons and daughters. It discourages friendships. It closes options for children who need parents to adopt and foster them. It separates children from their parents in custody battles. Anything that lessens prejudice against homosexuality will thus prevent considerable suffering for people of any sexuality.

As most children will be heterosexual when they grow up, the greatest gift a lesbian mother can give is freedom from prejudice and from the fear of homosexuality. Lesbian mothers cannot shield their children completely from exposure to homophobic prejudice nor inoculate them from its toxic effects but if the mothers are comfortable with and open about their lesbian identity, they should be in a strong position to provide a contrasting example and perspective to the predominant hostility towards homosexuality.

The sons and daughters of lesbians that I interviewed responded with positive attitudes towards homosexuality. They typically expressed the view that there is more than one acceptable sexual identity. Some expressed uneasiness with labels and the limits they impose on people's understanding of each other. Several spoke of their willingness to question their own sexuality. Their attitudes can be summed up by Kate, aged 24, who has both a lesbian mother and a gay father. She learned of her parents' sexuality when she was 15, soon after her mother became a lesbian.

> The main thing having gay parents has done is help me under-stand gay society and changed my view of gay people. There isn't that much to understand because they're normal people. It's just that they experience a lot of prejudice. If I hadn't had gay parents, I would have been carrying on like the rest of society, thinking they're in gay clubs and I'm not. I wouldn't really have understood.

Most of the respondents spoke of their willingness to assume responsibility for educating people out of their ignorance and preju-dice. Rachel, age 19, says,

> I've never had any stick at school about my Mum being les-bian. When people say to me, 'Is your mum gay?' I say, 'Yeah.' That's it. I'm not ashamed about it. It helps other people change their attitudes about gay people when they look at me and think, 'It's not such a weird thing, is it? Her mum is a lesbian and had children. She's a human being.'

For lesbian, bisexual and gay people, having an openly lesbian mother should make it easier for them to be comfortable with their sexuality than it is for those teenagers without such positive and intimate role models. Lesbian and gay people discover their sexual identity and seek out appropriate role models or communities regardless of their parents' sexuality or attitudes. A teenager with a lesbian mother should find this process easier, less painful and with less risk of parental rejection than a teenager with a heterosexual mother. The lesbian, gay and bisexual people I interviewed did perceive this as an advantage. For example, Rosie, age 20, is the bisexual daughter of a lesbian mother and a gay father. She says,

That my parents were gay made it a lot easier for me to come out and to see that there could be a physical dimension to my friendships with girls. I was encouraged to be what I wanted to be. I have experimented sexually, and my parents have created a supportive environment for that.

Emily, age 21, identifies as a lesbian and claims that,

having a lesbian mother has made it easier because there's an acceptable role model for me. Mum has always been my ally. For quite a while, she was the only out-lesbian that I knew.

There is some evidence to suggest that people raised by lesbian mothers are more open about sexuality than those raised by heterosexual parents. In a British comparative study of grown children, Golombok and Tasker (1996) found that the sons and daughters of the lesbian mothers were more likely to have considered and to have had same-sex sexual relationships when teenagers than the children of the heterosexual mothers. While similar proportions in each group reported sexual attraction to members of the same sex, it was the children of lesbians who felt able to act on their attraction. The authors reported that the young adults with lesbian mothers seemed to be more at ease in relation to talking about lesbian and gay issues. They concluded that parental attitudes towards sexuality must be one of the many influences on the development of an individual's sexual orientation but not a determining one.

WOMEN'S INDEPENDENCE

Another advantage noted by respondents was that they gained a tangible understanding of women's financial and emotional independence from men. Lesbian mothers, whether single or living as part of a couple, provide an alternative to the gender inequality so typical of heterosexual relationships. At best, lesbian mothers can demonstrate that women can function effectively and happily without male approval and support. At the least, lesbian mothers protect their children from the worst excesses of masculinity as they do not seek out or stay with violent and abusive men.

When asked to talk generally about the ways their mothers influenced them, several respondents volunteered the effect their mothers had on their views of gender relations. Katrina is at secondary school and is sharply critical of the gender relations between adolescent boys and girls. She comments,

> Other girls my age aren't able to hold their own because they've been brought up by dominating fathers. They can't stand up to boyfriends that bully them. My Mum is assertive and strong. She just won't be pushed around. I've learnt that from her. I've got confidence in myself. I'd say I'm more emotionally stable than many of my friends who are living with both their mum and dad.

Dissatisfied with her gay father's absence from her life, Kate says she prefers old-fashioned men who take charge and look after women. But she acknowledges her mother's alternative influence.

> My mother has strong opinions about domineering men and she is good at making me more independent and teaching me that life isn't so bad without a man. She doesn't always approve of the way I am with my boyfriends and is disappointed that I choose men so different from the people that she socializes with. I think she wants me to take a more leading role in my relationships with men, like the perfectly balanced equality she has had with her girlfriends. She hated my last boyfriend. When my mother criticized him to me, I began to think the way she did about him. That's when it finished. I'm glad I'm out of it and I'm a better person for it.

Mandy is a heterosexual woman raised by a lesbian mother. Her mother and father separated when she was one and her father had little to do with her as a child. At age 24, Mandy says,

> one of the meaningful things I've learned from Mum's relationships with her partners is to respect your own space and to be aware of other people's needs too. I see how Mum and her current partner give each other a tremendous amount of support. They are inseparable individuals in a very bonded rela-

tionship. But they respect their individuality. They can agree to disagree. I want a man who can hold me, who can talk to me, and . . . I want to have my space and independence noted and appreciated. I don't think I would have got that growing up in the heterosexual world. My values are all down to my Mum's choices.

Heterosexual couples have generally been slow to demonstrate equality and fairness in the allocation of domestic and childcare tasks (Dunne 1998), retaining the norm, a division based on gender. Men who take responsibility for caring for their children and the housework are the exception, noticed and praised precisely because of their rarity. Children growing up with parents who behave according to stereotypical role models also have such models of domestic life reinforced throughout the culture. The male and female roles modeled by most heterosexual parents are restrictive, leading to narrow definitions of human potential.

In contrast, there is a growing body of research indicating that lesbian couples are unlikely to be bound by such gendered thinking about parenting (Dunne 1998). Inequalities inevitably exist as a result of class, financial and personality differences but it is not common for lesbian couples with children to mimic heterosexual divisions of labour. Usually both partners in a lesbian partnership share the tasks of earning a living, caring for children and performing household chores. One North American study by Charlotte Patterson (1995) shows co-mothers (the mother without the biological connection) spending more time caring for their children than heterosexual birth fathers who live with their wives. In another North American study, David Flaks and his colleagues (1995) compared 15 lesbian couples who had children by donor insemination with 15 heterosexual couples. The lesbian couples were more aware of the skills needed for effective parenting than the heterosexual couples. They were better able to recognize problems in parenting and to envisage solutions for them. The heterosexual couples did less well in this comparison because the fathers performed poorly in this test. All the mothers, whether lesbian or heterosexual, were aware of good parenting skills. Gill Dunne (1996) compared 36 lesbian couples raising children with a national survey of heterosexual couples. The lesbian couples tended to have fairly equal involvement in domestic work and childcare resulting from their willingness and ability to find a balance between paid work and home life. Differences in time spent in paid work were less extreme in lesbian partnerships than heterosexual partnerships where gender divisions tend to limit men's parental role to providing for the family. As a result, lesbian couples have a head start over heterosexual couples for modelling equality in domestic life. Respondents cited this as influencing the egalitarianism that they achieved in their own relationships. Further research could explore this aspect further, as well as the domestic competence of sons of lesbians.

ATTITUDES TOWARDS THE CONCEPT OF FAMILY

The fact that there are lesbians with strong parental relationships to children despite their lack of legal and biological connections is a key development in the evolving conceptualizations of 'the family' and kinship. These bonds deserve legal recognition. Parenting is about caring and commitment, not just about the rights of adults to children. It is too easy to make a fetish of biological connections and dismiss relationships forged in the everyday reality of caring and loving.

Respondents were asked to explain who they counted as family, what family meant to them and what the circumstances were of their particular families. Their answers challenged fundamental aspects of traditional understandings of family, particularly the absolute and necessary link between biological kinship and family relationship. They counted people with no biological connection as family and did not include others with a biological bond. Family membership was earned by the quality of the relationship rather than by the mere sharing of genes.

An example is Katrina who is well aware that she shares half her genes with her father yet is under no illusions about his relationship to her. He abandoned the family when she was three and saw her and her brother intermittently despite her mother's desire that he be a responsible father. Katrina was not impressed when he appeared on her doorstep after having had no contact for four years. Nor was she pleased with the Happy Sixteenth card he sent on her fifteenth birthday. She says,

> I may have wished for a father figure in my life, but that was a dream really. I never had one. A dad is the word for the person that is the other half of my genetic make-up, but he's not my parent.

Family bonds develop where there are no biological relationships as when a birth mother with children starts a relationship with a new partner. These types of families are step-families, in many ways the same as the families created when heterosexual people divorce and remarry. A different kind of family is created, however, when one partner of a lesbian couple conceives by donor insemination and both raise the child. In a British study by Tasker and Golombok (in this volume), lesbian partners of mothers who conceived by donor insemination were more involved in parenting and more likely to see parenting as a shared enterprise than heterosexual couples. The difference was reduced though still apparent when the comparison was made with heterosexual parents who also had children by donor insemination.

The struggle for recognition as a valid type of family is the case for all step-families in Britain but heterosexual step-parents have the possibility of legal recognition of their role through marriage and adoption. For lesbian mothers without the biological connection, there are no public rituals confirming their membership in their family. Without the trappings of social legitimacy conferred by heterosexuality, the definition of family comes into sharper focus. As Katrina, 17, says,

> When I say family I use it as a broad term. A family includes anyone who's going to love and care for you unconditionally. That doesn't necessarily have to be your biological mother and father.

The descriptions of my respondents support the more inclusive definition proposed in a book about heterosexual step-families (Robinson & Smith 1993). They define a family as any group of people (and pets) that meets the needs of its members for growth and personal development, love and intimacy, caring and support, identity and sense of belonging. Members of this group are not restricted by number, age, sexuality, or gender or whether they live in the same household.

ACCEPTANCE OF DIVERSITY

Several writers have commented on acceptance of diversity as a positive outcome of lesbian parenting. Pennington (1987) suggested that children growing up with an appreciation for differences may have the potential for greater self-reliance and self-confidence. Patterson (1992) proposed that further research address the questions: 'Won't children of gays grow up with increased tolerance for difference? Won't they be more at home in multicultural environment?'

When asked to name advantages to having a lesbian mother, several of the people I interviewed suggested a greater acceptance of differences in lifestyles, types of families, cultures, religious beliefs, political views and values. For example, Mandy, a white woman, says,

> Mum's lesbianism and her strength of character have given me many choices in my life and so much freedom. She made me aware of racism and other important issues at a very young age.

Zoe, also white, says, 'I've been forced to think about things I might not have thought about otherwise, which I think is good. I think too many people just don't question anything.'

It seems logical that people who are accepting of sexual diversity will also be more accepting of diversity of any kind. There is reason to believe that the experience of one kind of oppression can generate greater awareness of other forms of oppression and greater acceptance of difference from the norm. In theory lesbian mothers should function in a moral and social framework which values diversity, stresses empathy with all oppressed people and allows children to determine for themselves what they value without pressure to conform to other people's values and expectations.

Not all lesbians are accepting of differences themselves and an experience of oppression does not guarantee empathy towards other oppressed people. Like anyone else, lesbians can be racist, intolerant of sexual diversity, dogmatic about their beliefs and insistent that their own lifestyle is the only correct one. It may be that the respondents who mentioned greater acceptance of diversity as an advantage were those whose mothers were not only lesbian but feminist. It would be interesting to pursue this question in systematic research studies and to tease out the influence of the parent's sexuality from that of her values and feminism.

CONCLUSION

Because the research on lesbian parenting has focused on children's adjustment and their gender development, it has missed potential advantages to children's development which could arise from having a lesbian mother. These are the moral and social values modeled by parents who are different from the norm. Whether they teach by example or by explanation, growing up with a lesbian mother should be a lesson in acceptance of diversity. Lesbian mothers who are comfortable with their sexuality model pride and self-acceptance. They can teach children to value diversity and to understand that there are many routes to happiness and self-fulfillment. To the extent that they act according to their own standards of right and wrong and challenge injustice and prejudice, they teach that 'people of integrity do not shrink from bigots' (quotation from judge in custody case, taken from Benkov, 1994). Most of all, they teach a view of the world that is more in keeping with 'reality,' a better preparation for life than the myths that most of us grow up with.

Today's children are growing up in a rapidly changing society where there are few certainties, no blueprints for living and a wealth of sexual identities, cultures, lifestyles, types of families and values. The most valuable lesson for children is to teach them to value diversity, to be empathic with people who are oppressed and not to be afraid of difference. They need to learn to determine for themselves what they value and how they are going to live their lives. Having a lesbian mother may well be one of the ways to learn these lessons.

REFERENCES

Benkov, Laura (1994) *Reinventing the Family–the emerging story of lesbian and gay parents*, New York: Crown Publishers.

Dunne, Gillian A (1998) '"Pioneers behind our own front doors," new models for the organization of work in partnerships' *Work Employment and Society*, March.

Dunne, Gillian A (1996) 'Why can't a man be more like a woman? In search of balanced domestic and employment lives,' unpublished report.

Flaks, David, Ficher, Ilda, Masterpasqua, Frank, Joseph, Gregory (1995) 'Lesbians choosing motherhood: a comparative study of lesbian and heterosexual parents and their children,' *Developmental Psychology*, 31(1):105-14.

Golombok, Susan and Tasker, Fiona (1996) 'Do parents influence the sexual orientation of their children? Findings from a longitudinal study of lesbian families,' *Developmental Psychology*, 32(1):1-9.

Golombok, Susan and Tasker, Fiona (1997) *Growing up in a lesbian family–effects on child development*, New York, London: The Guilford Press.

Patterson, Charlotte (1992) 'Children of Lesbian and Gay Parents,' *Child Development*, 63:1025-42.

Patterson, Charlotte (1995) 'Families of the lesbian baby boom: parents' division of labor and children's adjustment,' *Developmental Psychology*, 31(1):115-23.

Pennington, Saralie Bisnovich (1987) 'Children of Lesbian Mothers,' in Frederick W. Bozett (ed.), *Gay and Lesbian Parents*, NY, London: Praeger.

Robinson, Margaret and Smith, Donna (1993) *Step by Step-focus on stepfamilies*. Herts: Harvester Wheatsheaf.

Saffron, Lisa (1996) *What about the children? Sons and Daughters of lesbians and gay men speak about their lives*. London: Cassell.

Wellings, Kaye, Julia Field, Anne M Johnson, Jane Wadsworth (1994) Chapter 5 'Sexual diversity and homosexual behaviour' in *Sexual Behaviour in Britain–The National Survey of Sexual Attitudes and Lifestyles*, Penguin.

The Role of Co-Mothers
in Planned Lesbian-Led Families

Fiona Tasker
Susan Golombok

SUMMARY. The present study examined the role of co-parents in children's lives by comparing the role of co-mothers in 15 British lesbian mother families with the role of resident fathers in two different groups of heterosexual families (43 families where the study-child was conceived through donor insemination, and 41 families where the child had been naturally conceived). Birth mothers in all

Fiona Tasker, PhD, is Lecturer in Psychology at Birkbeck College, University of London. She completed her PhD at the University of Cambridge, and was a postdoctoral research fellow at City University, London. Her previous publications include papers on children of divorce and children in lesbian and gay families.

Susan Golombok, PhD, is Professor of Psychology and Director of the Family and Child Psychology Research Centre at City University, London. She has published widely on the influence of nontraditional families on children's development.

Address correspondence to Fiona Tasker, PhD, Department of Psychology, Birkbeck College, University of London, Malet Street, London, WC1E 7HX, UK.

The authors would like to thank Clare Murray for her help in interviewing families and Gill Dunne for her comments on this paper. The authors also wish to acknowledge the support of the Medical Research Council who funded the project on which this paper is based.

Portions of this article were presented at the annual meeting of the British Psychological Society Developmental Section, September 1996, Oxford, England.

[Haworth co-indexing entry note]: "The Role of Co-Mothers in Planned Lesbian-Led Families." Tasker, Fiona, and Susan Golombok. Co-published simultaneously in *Journal of Lesbian Studies* (The Haworth Press, Inc.) Vol. 2, No. 4, 1998, pp. 49-68; and: *Living "Difference": Lesbian Perspectives on Work and Family Life* (ed: Gillian A. Dunne) The Haworth Press, Inc., 1998, pp. 49-68; and: *Living "Difference": Lesbian Perspectives on Work and Family Life* (ed: Gillian A. Dunne) Harrington Park Press, an imprint of The Haworth Press, Inc., 1998, pp. 49-68. Single or multiple copies of this article are available for a fee from The Haworth Document Delivery Service [1-800-342-9678, 9:00 a.m. - 5:00 p.m. (EST). E-mail address: getinfo@haworthpressinc.com].

49

three types of family were administered a semi-structured interview to assess the quality of family relationships. Questionnaire data on stress associated with parenting were obtained from co-mothers and fathers, and the children were administered the Family Relations Test. The results indicated that co-mothers played a more active role in daily caretaking than did most fathers. However, father-child and co-mother-child relationships were found to be equally warm and affectionate in all three groups and no group differences were found for children's scores on the Family Relations Test or co-mothers/fathers' scores on the Parenting Stress Index. *[Article copies available for a fee from The Haworth Document Delivery Service: 1-800-342-9678. E-mail address: getinfo@haworthpressinc.com]*

INTRODUCTION

In North America and Western Europe, including Britain, there has been increasing academic interest among developmental psychologists in parenting in nontraditional families. Recent studies of children brought up by lesbian mothers have begun to examine the role of nonbiological mothers (co-mothers) in bringing up children. For example, it has been shown that young adults brought up by their lesbian mother after their parents divorced generally report good relationships with their mother's female partner, and when compared with young adults who had been brought up by their mother and stepfather, are more positive about their mother's female partner (Tasker & Golombok, 1995; Tasker & Golombok, 1997). Saffron (this volume) also suggests that adolescent and adult children of lesbian mothers may hold wider and more inclusive definitions of family compared with those held by other young people.

Recent studies have examined how well children fare in planned lesbian-led families. Several studies in Europe and North America have found that school-age children conceived through donor insemination (DI) and brought up from birth by either a lesbian couple or single lesbian mother show good adjustment on a variety of psychological measures (Brewaeys et al., in press; Chan et al., 1998; Flaks et al., 1995; Golombok et al., 1997; Patterson, 1994). It seems to be family processes (such as family conflict), rather than family structure (parental sexual orientation and number of parents), that have the greater influence on children's psychological adjustment. Children do best in lesbian and heterosexual families where parents report greater relationship satisfaction and little conflict, and lower levels of parenting stress (Chan et al., 1998). When compared directly with fathers in heterosexual two-parent families, co-mothers showed a greater awareness of necessary parenting skills (Flaks et al., 1995), and were more involved on a day-to-day basis with their children (Brewaeys et al., in press; Dunne, in press, a; Patterson, 1995).

Previous studies have often lacked appropriate heterosexual family comparison groups to control for the important factors associated with lesbian parenthood through DI. Firstly, the absence of a genetic relationship with the child's second parent needs to be considered. Secondly, undergoing donor insemination can be complicated and stressful. Finally, perhaps the most important factor to consider is that lesbian mothers have often gone to great lengths to have a much-wanted child. These issues also are relevant to heterosexual couples using DI to conceive a child. One study of children conceived with the aid of new reproductive technologies and raised by heterosexual parents found that both mothers and fathers were more involved in parenting if their child had been conceived either through DI or through IVF (in vitro fertilization) than were parents of the children in the naturally conceived control group (Golombok et al., 1995).

In Britain many lesbian women use self-insemination to conceive a child rather than the services of fertility clinics. While British fertility clinics can legally provide services for lesbian women, the influential Warnock Report leading to the Human Fertilization and Embryology Act (1990) was not supportive of lesbian parenting, claiming that it is in the child's best interest to have both a mother and a father. Other factors that have prevented, or discouraged, lesbian women from using fertility clinics have been the financial cost of donor insemination (especially as several inseminations may be needed before a pregnancy is achieved with frozen semen), the wish of many women to have a known donor who may or may not develop a relationship with the child, and the desire to remain in control of conception and pregnancy which could be jeopardized by the medicalization of treatment at a clinic (Saffron, 1994).

Other methodological criticisms have been levied at existing research, namely the reliance on small self-selected samples of lesbian-led families and the absence of corroborating data from more than one family member. In particular, previous research on children born to lesbian mothers has not examined the quality of family relationships as viewed by the biological mothers, co-mothers and children.

In the present study, involvement of co-mothers in childcare in lesbian-led families was compared with that of fathers in both heterosexual families where the child had been naturally conceived (NC) and in heterosexual families where the child had been conceived through donor insemination (DI), thus controlling for factors associated with this assisted reproduction technique. The quality of family relationships was also assessed in all three family types. It was hypothesized that co-mothers in lesbian-led families would be more involved in childcare than fathers in heterosexual families, and that this would positively influence the quality of the co-parent's relationship with her child. However, differences between co-mothers and fathers in heterosexual families with a child conceived through DI were predicted to be less pronounced, because children had been planned for and greatly desired in both types of donor insemination family.

METHOD

Participants

Lesbian-led families (L). Fifteen families led by a cohabiting lesbian couple (with a total of 5 sons and 10 daughters aged between 3-9 years old) were identified from a wider group of thirty lesbian-led families. This British nationwide volunteer sample had been recruited to the project via advertisements in newsletters and contacts within the lesbian community. All of the birth mothers and co-mothers were white. Fourteen of the lesbian couples had conceived their child through donor insemination to one of the mothers (in 11 cases by self-insemination). In the remaining case the child was conceived in a heterosexual relationship which had ended before the child's birth. In all 15 cases the child had been brought up in a lesbian-headed home since birth. In 10 cases the birth mother and co-mother had been cohabiting prior to the child's birth and had planned parenthood together. In five cases the birth-mother and the co-parent were not in a living-together relationship at the time of the child's birth; nevertheless they were cohabiting and parenting together at the time of the study (1993-1994). Five of the fifteen co-mothers also were the biological mother of an older or younger child not included in this study.

Heterosexual families. The role of co-mothers was compared with the role of fathers in two different heterosexual family groups. Both groups of two-parent heterosexual families had been recruited as part of a larger study of assisted reproduction families (Golombok et al., 1995). The heterosexual family groups are as follows: (i) 41 families recruited from maternity ward records where the child had been naturally conceived and was being brought up by both biological parents (NC), and (ii) 43 families where the child had been conceived by anonymous donor insemination via a fertility clinic and was being brought up by both parents (DI). For both types of heterosexual family recruited from hospital and clinic records the participation rate was 62%.

There was a similar proportion of boys and girls in each group of families (Chi-square = 2.38; df = 2; NS). Across all three groups the average age of children in the study was 6 years old. However, the oldest children in the study tended to be from the two-parent lesbian families (mean age six-and-a-half years) while the youngest children tended to be from the heterosexual DI families (mean age five-and-a-half years) (F[2,96] = 5.76; p < 0.01). Significant group differences also were found in respect of the following variables: social class of the highest earner (using the UK Registrar General's classification of occupations), age of mother, and number of children in the family. With respect to social class there was a higher proportion of working class families among the two-parent heterosexual donor insemination families than among the other family types (Chi-square = 27.54; df = 6; p < 0.0001). With respect to the age of the birth mothers, the lesbian mothers were the oldest (average [mean] age 40 years and 5 months at the time of interview), followed by the heterosexual mothers with a naturally conceived child (mean age 40 years), and the heterosexual mothers with a child conceived by donor insemination (mean age 36 years) were the youngest (F[2,96] = 12.10; p < 0.0001). No significant group differences were found with respect to the age of the co-mother or father. However, the groups significantly differed in family size, with fewer children in the lesbian-led group (Chi-square = 9.76; df = 4; p < 0.05). Therefore, social class, the age of the birth mother, family size, and the age of the study child were entered as covariates into subsequent statistical analyses (effectively controlling for these differences).

Measures

Birth mother's reports of co-mother's or father's involvement in childcare. All the families were visited at home on at least two occasions. On the first visit the birth mother took part in an individual interview and a self-report questionnaire was completed by the birth mother and co-mother or father. In some cases the questionnaires were returned by post, with over 90% of questionnaires returned for analysis. On the second visit, data were collected from the child. Birth mothers in all three types of family were interviewed about family relationships for one-and-a-half hours on average using an adaptation of a semi-structured interview on parenting quality (Quinton & Rutter, 1988). The original interview has been validated against home observations of the mother-child relationship, revealing a high level of agreement between interviewers' ratings of parenting and the observational data.

From this interview specific ratings were made of the following variables used in the present investigation. The extent to which the co-mother or father took the load in parenting (*parenting load*) was rated on a 5-point scale from "0"-"no involvement" to "4"-"major parenting load." This took into account information on the involvement of the co-mother or father in daily childcare (e.g., being at home for the child, preparing meals, taking the child to and from nursery or school). The involvement of the co-mother and father in disciplinary interactions (*parental coordination of discipline*) was also assessed and the degree to which the couple coordinated discipline was rated on a 5-point scale from "0"-"active uncoordination" to "4"-"coordinated action." This took into account information in response to questions concerning both parents' responses to disciplinary issues with the child that had occurred over the three months prior to the interview.

The extent to which co-mother/father showed affection to the child (*co-mother/father expressed affection towards child*) and received affection from the child (*child's expressed affection towards co-mother/father*) were rated on 4-point scales from "0"-"little or none" to "4"-"a great deal." Information for rating these variables was taken from responses to questions pertaining to the extent to which there was demonstrable warmth between parent and child, such that each showed spontaneous affection or verbally expressed a positive regard for the other.

The extent to which co-mother/father enjoyed playing with the child (*co-mother/father enjoyment of play*) also was rated on 4-point scales from "0"-"little or none" to "4"-"a great deal." The information for this variable was gleaned from responses to questions about the types of play activities parents and children engaged in together, including whether the co-parent and father prioritized play activities, and enjoyed actively participating in them, or instead merely supervised activities.

A global rating was also made by the trained interviewer of the co-parent's or father's overall involvement with the child (*global rating of co-parent/father's involvement in parenting*), taking into account the extent to which the co-mother/father took responsibility for the child and the quality of her or his relationship with the child (rated on a 5-point scale from "0"-"very low" to "4"-"very high").

Most of the co-mothers in the lesbian-led families were also interviewed using the same interview as the birth mothers. Fathers in heterosexual families were not interviewed as this had not been possible in the earlier study of children in heterosexual families conceived by assisted reproduction techniques. Consequently, no direct comparisons can be made between co-mothers and fathers on these interview data. An interview from one of the co-mothers is quoted in one of the case studies given below to illustrate the diversity of parenting experiences in lesbian-led families.

Parenting Stress Index [PSI]. The short form of the Parenting Stress Index (Abidin, 1990) was administered to co-mothers and fathers. This measure gives a total score of the general level of parenting stress an individual is experiencing (*PSI total score*), together with three sub-scale scores of (i) *parental distress* (encompassing feelings of parental incompetence, stresses associated with restrictions on lifestyle, conflict with the child's other parent, lack of social support, and depression), (ii) *parent-child dysfunctional interaction* (reflecting the parent's perception that the child does not match up to expectations and that interactions with the child are not enjoyable), and (iii) *difficult child* (the behavioural characteristics of children that make them easy or difficult to manage). Test-retest reliability for the PSI has been shown to be high over a 6-month period, demonstrating consistency in measurement. Concurrent and predictive validity also have been demonstrated for the full-length questionnaire, and the short form is highly correlated with the full-length version (Abidin, 1990).

Family Relations Test. The Family Relations Test (Bene & Anthony, 1985) was administered to the children to obtain a standardized assessment of the child's feelings about their parents. From a set of cut-out figures mounted on small cardboard boxes, children from lesbian families chose an imaginary birth mother and co-mother, and children from heterosexual families chose an imaginary mother and father. These figures were placed in front of the child together with a neutral figure, "Mr Nobody." The child was then given a set of cards with emotional messages printed on each (e.g., [child] thinks you are nice) and was asked to post each of the cards into the box of the person for whom they felt the card was most appropriate. The test was scored to produce a measure of positive feelings and a measure of negative feelings from each parent to the child, and from the child to each parent. If the child selected two people to receive a particular card, a score of one half was given to each so that the total amount of each characteristic given remained the same for each child. In the present investigation, the scores were combined to give a global rating (*child's perception of their relationship with co-mother/father*) of the extent of positive feelings between the child and co-mother or father [(positive feelings to co-mother/father + positive feelings from co-mother/father) – (negative feelings to co-mother/father + negative feelings from co-mother/father)]. The higher the score the more positive the feelings. Acceptable test-retest reliability for the Family Relations Test has been demonstrated with children of two-parent heterosexual families, and validation studies have shown the test to discriminate between clinical and non-clinical groups of children (Bean, 1976; Kaufman et al., 1972; Philip & Orr, 1978).

RESULTS

Birth Mothers' Reports of the Co-Mother's or Father's Relationship with the Child and Involvement in Parenting

With the data collected for this study we had the opportunity to do statistical analyses (one-way analysis of co-variance [ANCOVA]) which enabled us to examine parent-child relationships in the lesbian and heterosexual-headed homes while partialling out any of the differences in scores that were related to differences outlined previously between the families in terms of the birth mother's age, the study child's age, social class and family size. The details of the statistical analyses conducted are presented next for the interested reader. One-way ANCOVA's using type of family [group] as the between-subjects variable (and the birth mother's age, study child's age, social class of family, and family size as co-variates) were conducted for each of the variables assessed in the birth mother's interview. Where a significant group difference was found, independent contrasts were conducted to examine specific issues. These were: (i) *lesbian family vs. heterosexual family* [L vs. NC] to examine whether the co-mother's role in lesbian-led families is different from the father's role in families led by two heterosexual parents, (ii) *lesbian family vs. heterosexual DI family* [L vs. DI] to examine whether any differences in parenting roles remained when the issues associated with donor insemination had been controlled for.

Comparing birth mothers' reports across the three family groups of the co-mother's or heterosexual father's involvement in parenting indicated that co-mothers were more involved in parenting than fathers, especially when compared with fathers in families who had not conceived their child via donor insemination (see Figure 1). A significant difference was found between groups for the global rating of co-mother's/father's involvement in parenting ($F[2,90] = 11.30$, $p < 0.0001$). Planned contrast analyses revealed that co-mothers in lesbian-led families were more involved in parenting

FIGURE 1. Parenting Involvement

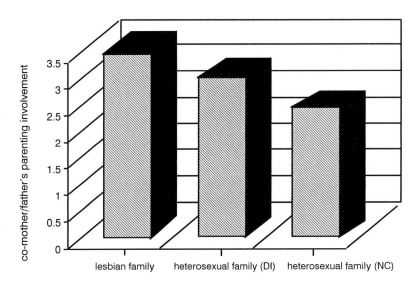

generally than were fathers in the heterosexual two-parent families (User contrast [L vs. NC], t = 4.72, p < 0.0001), while this difference was reduced (although not eliminated) when lesbian co-parents were compared with fathers in the heterosexual DI family group (User contrast [L vs. DI], t = 2.16, p < 0.05).

In order to examine underlying differences in parenting that were associated with co-mothers' involvement in parenting, several particular aspects of parenting were considered next: (i) playing with child, (ii) showing and receiving the child's affection, (iii) role in daily caregiving. No differences between the lesbian or heterosexual family groups were found in the extent to which co-mothers or fathers were reported to enjoy playing with the study child (F[2,85] = 0.99, NS), the co-mother's or father's expressed affection towards child (F[2,89] = 0.44, NS), or the child's expressed affection towards their co-mother or father (F[2,90] = 0.59, NS).

However, co-mothers were more likely than fathers in either type of heterosexual family to take a major role in daily caregiving (see Figure 2). In terms of the distribution of 'parenting load' in the

FIGURE 2. Parenting Load

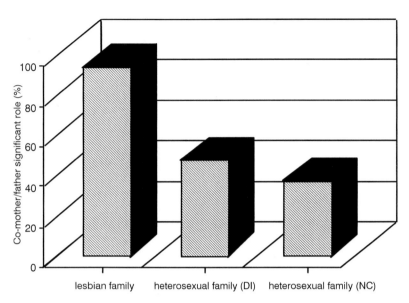

different types of family, over 90% (14/15) of the co-mothers were reported by birth mothers to be at least as involved as the birth mother herself in parenting (i.e., taking a significant parenting load), compared with 20/43 (47%) of fathers in families with a child conceived by DI, and 15/41 (37%) of fathers with a naturally conceived child (Chi-square = 14.42, df = 2, p < 0.001).

Differences in the way that parents agreed or disagreed about disciplining their daughter or son (parental coordination of discipline) in each type of family may also be indicative of the relatively greater involvement of co-mothers in lesbian-led families in daily childcare compared with that reported for the majority of fathers in heterosexual two-parent families. Sixty percent (9/15) of lesbian-led families had a joint or coordinated policy on disciplining their son or daughter, compared with 22% (9/41) of heterosexual families with a naturally conceived child, and 23% (10/43) of heterosexual families with a child conceived through DI (Chi-square = 9.95; df = 4; p < 0.05).

Parenting Stress Index (PSI)

Co-mothers in lesbian-led families and fathers in either type of heterosexual family did not differ on their reported levels of parenting stress on the Parenting Stress Index (PSI). One-way ANCOVA's with one between-subjects variable [group], and birth mother's age, study child's age, social class of family, and family size as co-variates, were conducted with the total score on the co-mother's or father's PSI and each of the PSI subscales as dependent variables. No group differences were found in the extent of co-mother's or father's total PSI scores ($F[2,66] = 0.12$; NS), parental distress subscale ($F[2,66] = 1.53$; NS), difficult child subscale ($F[2,66] = 0.23$, NS), or parent-child dysfunctional interaction subscale ($F[2,66] = 0.06$, NS).

Family Relations Test

Across the different types of family children had similar perceptions of the warmth of their relationship with their co-mother in the lesbian-led families or with their father in either of the two types of heterosexual family. A similar one-way ANCOVA was carried out for the child's score on the Family Relations Test. No group difference was found in the children's perception of the quality of their relationship with their co-mother or father ($F2,75) = 2.38$, NS).

CASE STUDIES

We have concentrated on presenting the average pattern of parenting across the different family groups, although there were of course many different ways of organizing parenting within each type of family. The following case studies have been selected because they best illustrate the main findings from our interviews and give some idea of the diversity of parenting within the lesbian-led families. In order to respect confidentiality we have changed the names of family members in these extracts.

Case Study 1

Cleo and Wendy had lived together for three years prior to Cleo conceiving their son Jonathan through donor insemination at a fertility clinic. Jonathan was five years old at the time the family participated in this research. The following extract from Cleo's interview illustrates the importance she gives to Wendy's role as Jonathan's co-mother.

Interviewer: And how would you describe Wendy's relationship with Jonathan, are they affectionate to one another?

Cleo: Oh absolutely, yeah. I mean they're extremely attached to one another.

Interviewer: Would Jonathan go up to Wendy for cuddles?

Cleo: Not as much as he would to me. But he certainly would. I mean if there's a choice between [us] he would go to me. But he would also go to Wendy in all sorts of other circumstances. I mean very similar as you'd see in most other households with two parents, that children will often go to their mother in those situations. So it's very similar to that. I mean I can think of no families that I know where that's not the case, you know in heterosexual households.

And later in the same interview:

Interviewer: How would you say that Jonathan's relationship with you and his relationship with Wendy differ?

Cleo: I see it in terms of like that he has the primary relationship with me and Wendy's like the secondary parent. I mean similar to sort of mothers and fathers, you know that mothers are often primary. I know I'm sounding incredibly traditional here, don't I? [laughs]. I mean she is as significant. I mean she's his other parent. I mean he's got two parents . . . I mean all I'm trying to say really is that it's very similar to most other households with two parents whether they're heterosexual or not. And it's not, what it's not is like a lot of lesbian households where there's a sort of two mothers thing. It's not that. It's definitely a sort of primary mother relationship and a relationship with the other parent. But Wendy is involved in lots and lots of the day to day detail of his life, you know the practical stuff.

Interviewer: OK, does Wendy look after him at times when you're not around?
Cleo: Oh lots.

Interviewer: On what sort of occasions?
Cleo: Well three days a week she would have him. She either picks him up from school, or picks him up when he goes for very short periods to his childminder. . . . So Wendy is looking after him three days a week after school and I do the two days. And every day there would be detailed involvement with both of us.

Case Study 2

Miriam and Debbie also had been together for a similar length of time before Stephen (age 3 years old) was born. Debbie had given birth to Stephen after conceiving through self-insemination. Stephen's biological father occasionally visits Stephen and his mothers, but he has no involvement in parenting. Stephen calls his birth mother Debbie "mummy" and his co-mother Miriam "Miri." The following extracts are taken from Miriam's interview.

Interviewer: What's Stephen's personality like?
Miriam: Um, he's a good natured child, he's very enjoyable so he's easy to talk to about things. So you know he's not one of those that his immediate reaction is to cry if he can't do something. He's quite good.

Interviewer: Well that's given me some idea of what he's like–
Miriam: Oh he's loveable.

Interviewer: Do you find him easy to be affectionate with?
Miriam: Oh God yes! He's loveable. . . . He'll just come round and say "Can I have a cuddle?" Or if we're sitting having a meal he'll put his arms up.

Interviewer: And would Stephen be affectionate with Debbie as well?
Miriam: Oh yes.

Interviewer: Would he be keener on you or keener on her?
Miriam: No he doesn't actually play us off against each other. I
            mean if he's upset, really upset, he might say "I want
            my Miri" if he's with Debbie, or "I want my
            mummy" if he's with me. Or if he's with both of us
            he'll say "I want my daddy" and then we say "Well
            what good will that do for you Stevie?"

Later in the interview a question about how often Miriam plays with
Stephen indicates the amount of time she spends looking after him.

Interviewer: How often would you do a puzzle or a game with him?
Miriam: Well I have him all day Saturday, or most of Saturday
            [when Debbie's working] so we'll do whatever. Well,
            we go to the park on Saturday and then we come back
            here and play. And we play dozens of games then. And
            then 'cause I have flexi-time as well you see, so when
            he comes home [from nursery], he comes back home
            with Debbie, and they get here about half-past-four,
            and if I'm here then I'll play with him. But if I'm not
            [home], because I've not got back yet, she'll play with
            him. So it's after nursery too it's that sort of time. Well
            I don't know, it's always on a Saturday and often on a
            Sunday if we don't go out [as a family]. And it's got to
            be at least three or four times a week.

DISCUSSION

The results of this research showed that co-mothers in lesbian-led
families played a more active role in daily caregiving than did most
fathers in heterosexual families, although this difference was often
less pronounced in heterosexual families where the child had been
conceived by donor insemination. However, data from both the
birth mother and the child on the closeness of co-mother or father-
child relationships indicated that family relationships were equally
warm and affectionate in all three groups. Furthermore, questionnaire data from the Parenting Stress Index showed no group differences in stress associated with parenting as reported by co-mothers
and fathers.

It is possible that the volunteer sample of lesbian-led families recruited for the study may have resulted in a bias toward families without problems, although this bias may apply also to the heterosexual family groups as some families declined our invitation to participate in the study. Given that many lesbians are not able to be "out" about their sexual orientation, recruiting a representative sample of lesbian-led families is unrealistic. Since the majority of data on the role of co-mothers and fathers in all three types of family was obtained from birth mothers, the possibility also remains that, compared with the heterosexual mothers in the study, the lesbian mothers may have wished to portray a more positive picture of their partner's involvement in childcare given the lack of public recognition of female co-parents.

Notwithstanding the above caveats, the findings from the present study emphasize the involvement of female co-parents in daily childcare. As such these results complement the conclusions of other researchers (Brewaeys et al., in press; Dunne, 1998a; Patterson, 1995). It seems likely that the greater commitment to equality in childcare responsibilities noted in other studies of lesbian parents has influenced the lesbian couples in the present study. Findings from other studies suggest that equality in partnership is not just confined to lesbian couples with children (Dunne, 1997). Furthermore, another study of the division of household labour between childless couples found that lesbian couples were more likely than either gay or heterosexual couples to share housework (Kurdek, 1993). Similarly Blumstein and Schwartz (1983) point to the greater emphasis placed by lesbian couples on equality compared with gay male couples, and especially heterosexual couples.

It is also fruitful to take a broader view in examining the relationship between lesbian partners and how parenthood interacts with each woman's career. This perspective suggests that the balance between commitment to paid work and parenting is facilitated by the absence of gender polarization and a similar understanding of the opportunities and challenges that women face in the workplace and in motherhood (Dunne, 1998a; 1998b). Among the mainly middle-class group of lesbian couples with children in Dunne's research, domestic work tends to be evenly balanced, and although co-mothers were more likely than their partners to be employed full-time, they appeared less likely than highly qualified fathers to be in full-time paid employment. The implication of this for the present discussion is that co-mothers may be more willing than most fathers to compromise paid-work in order to take on more involvement in daily parenting.

In the present investigation, the generally greater involvement in caregiving of co-mothers in lesbian-led families than most fathers does not seem to be simply a product of the extent to which the child was planned for as reflected by the use of donor insemination, although controlling for the use of DI does seem to account for some of the difference in father/co-parent involvement. There were however no group differences in the quality of family relationships between the child and their co-mother or the father. The absence of a genetic relationship between the co-mother or father and the child in both lesbian mother families and heterosexual families where the child had been conceived by DI seemingly did not affect the quality of the co-mother/father-child relationship for children in this age group.

Planning for shared parenthood through DI may entail different considerations for lesbian couples than for heterosexual couples. Most heterosexual couples who have DI will have been trying unsuccessfully to have a baby for some time and will have probably used DI as a "last resort" (Humphrey & Humphrey, 1988). While the couple will have had to think through how much they want to have a child, and whether they are willing to use donor semen in order to achieve this, they will not necessarily have needed to think carefully through future parenting roles given the abundance of models of heterosexual parenting. In contrast, lesbian couples will have spent time deciding which partner will become pregnant, or who first, and what level of commitment the other partner will make to the child and the birth mother. These discussions necessitate a more in-depth consideration of expectations regarding relative parenting roles and responsibilities within the lesbian-led family in a way which heterosexual couples are less likely to consider (Hargaden & Llewellin, 1996), and possibly lead on to a high level of involvement in childcare on the part of the co-mother after the baby's birth.

It is intriguing that the greater involvement of co-mothers in childcare compared with most fathers is not paralleled by increased closeness in the quality of the co-mother-child relationship as reported by either the birth mother or the child. Perhaps higher levels of involvement in childcare would have a greater impact on the co-mother's own report of her relationship with the child, a possibility that remains to be investigated. It is also possible that in the lesbian-led families the absence of gender differences between parents meant that children viewed both their mothers in a similar way and consequently gave more "half" cards to the symbolic figures in the Family Relations Test compared with children in either type of heterosexual family. This artefact of the scoring system may have disproportionately reduced scores of the co-mothers. However, accepting the results as they stand, it may be the case that the "second" parent's involvement in childcare and the quality of the parent-child relationship are not connected in families such as those in the present study where there is a high level of childcare generally within the home. Alternatively, increased involvement in childcare may not be associated with changes in the quality of the parent-child relationship until later in the child's life. Certainly the follow-up interviews with the young adults raised by lesbian mothers who took part in the British Longitudinal Study of Lesbian Mother Families (Tasker & Golombok, 1997) suggest that by adulthood children from lesbian-led stepfamilies have in general formed very close relationships with their mother's partner.

In summary, the results of this study point to the important role that co-mothers in lesbian two-parent families play in children's lives. Furthermore, the results indicate that the quality of the child's relationship with their "second" parent appears to be unrelated to whether that parent is female or male.

REFERENCES

Abidin, R. (1990). *Parenting Stress Index Test Manual.* Charlottesville, VA: Pediatric Psychology Press.

Bean, B.W. (1976). *An Investigation of the Reliability and Validity of the Family Relations Test.* Unpublished doctoral thesis, University of Kansas.

Bene, E. & Anthony, J. (1985) *Manual for the Family Relations Test.* Windsor, UK: NFER-NELSON.

Blumstein, P. & Schwartz, P. (1983). *American Couples*. New York: Morrow.

Brewaeys, A., Ponjaert, I., van Hall, E. & Golombok, S. (in press). Donor Insemination: Child Development and Family Functioning in Lesbian Mother Families with 4-8 Year Old Children. *Human Reproduction*.

Chan, R.W., Raboy, B. & Patterson, C.J. (1998). Psychosocial adjustment among children conceived via donor insemination by lesbian and heterosexual mothers. *Child Development, 69,* 443-457.

Dunne, G.A. (1997). *Lesbian lifestyles: Women's work and the politics of sexuality*. London: MacMillan.

Dunne, G.A. (1998a). 'Pioneers behind our own front doors': New models for the organization of work in domestic partnerships. *Work, Employment & Society*.

Dunne, G.A. (1998b). A passion for 'sameness'?: Sexuality and gender accountability. In C. Smart & E. Silva (eds.) *The 'New' Family?* London: Sage.

Flaks, D.K., Ficher, I., Masterpasqua, F., & Joseph, G. (1995) Lesbians choosing motherhood: A comparative study of lesbian and heterosexual parents and their children. *Developmental Psychology, 31,* 105-114.

Golombok, S., Cook, R., Bish, A., & Murray, C. (1995). Families created by the new reproductive technologies: Quality of parenting and social and emotional development of the children. *Child Development, 66,* 285-298.

Golombok, S. Tasker, F., & Murray, C. (1997). Children raised in fatherless families from infancy: Family relationships and the socioemotional development of children of lesbian and single heterosexual mothers. *Journal of Child Psychology & Psychiatry, 38,* 783-791.

Hargaden, H. & Llewellin, S. (1996). Lesbian and gay parenting issues. In D. Davies & C. Neal (Eds) *Pink Therapy: A Guide for Counsellors and Therapists Working with Lesbian, Gay and Bisexual Clients* (pp. 116-130). Milton Keynes, UK: Open University Press.

Humphrey, M. & Humphrey, H. (1988). *Families with a Difference: Varieties of Surrogate Parenthood*. London: Routledge.

Kaufman, J.M., Weaver, S.J. & Weaver, A. (1972). Family Relations Test responses of retarded readers: Reliability and comparative data. *Journal of Personality Assessment, 36,* 353-360.

Kurdek, L.A. (1993). The Allocation of Household Labor in Gay, Lesbian, and Heterosexual Married Couples. *Journal of Social Issues, 49,* 127-139.

Patterson, C.J. (1994). Children of the lesbian baby boom: Behavioral adjustment, self-concepts, and sex-role identity. In B. Greene & G. Herek (Eds.), *Contemporary perspectives on lesbian and gay psychology: Theory, research and application* (pp. 156-175). Beverly Hills, CA: Sage.

Patterson, C.J. (1995). Families of the lesbian baby boom: Parents' division of labor and children's adjustment. *Developmental Psychology, 31,* 115-123.

Philip, R.L. & Orr, R.R. (1978). Family Relations as perceived by emotionally disturbed and normal boys. *Journal of Personality Assessment, 42,* 121-127.

Quinton, D. & Rutter, M. (1988). *Parenting breakdown: The making and breaking of intergenerational links*. Aldershot: Avebury Gower Publishing.

Saffron, L. (1994). *Challenging Conceptions: Planning a Family by Self-insemination*. London: Cassell.

Tasker, F. & Golombok, S. (1995). Adults raised as children in lesbian families. *American Journal of Orthopsychiatry, 65*, 203-215.

Tasker, F. & Golombok, S. (1997). *Growing up in a lesbian family: Effects on Child Development*. New York: Guilford.

Reclaiming the 'Housewife'?
Lesbians and Household Work

Sarah Oerton

SUMMARY. This article addresses the contention that some research on household work in non-heterosexual households has been characterized by a tendency to 'empty' such households of any processes and practices associated with gendering. As a result, lesbians, particularly in co-residing, couple households, have been seen as having more egalitarian, democratic divisions of household labour. This article takes issue with such analyses and argues for the central importance of gender in constituting the organization of work in and between lesbians' households and kin networks. In particular, it addresses the contention that although gender difference may be less obvious in lesbian household arrangements, the issue of who gender

Sarah Oerton is Lecturer in Sociology and Women's Studies at the University of Glamorgan, South Wales, U.K. She researches and teaches in the areas of family, gender and sexuality; work and organizational life; social exclusion and social inequalities. Her most recent book is *Beyond Hierarchy: Gender, Sexuality and the Social Economy* (Taylor and Francis, 1996).

Address correspondence to Sarah Oerton, School of Humanities and Social Sciences, University of Glamorgan, Pontypridd, Mid Glamorgan, CF37 1DL, U.K. (e-mail: SOERTON@glam.ac.uk).

The author would like to thank Jo Van Every for her input into the early stages of the framing of her ideas, and to offer special thanks to Gillian Dunne and Jo Phoenix for their constructive comments on later versions. She is also grateful to all of her 'family' for the huge amount of support they have given her over many years.

[Haworth co-indexing entry note]: "Reclaiming the 'Housewife'? Lesbians and Household Work." Oerton, Sarah. Co-published simultaneously in *Journal of Lesbian Studies* (The Haworth Press, Inc.) Vol. 2, No. 4, 1998, pp. 69-83; and: *Living "Difference": Lesbian Perspectives on Work and Family Life* (ed: Gillian A. Dunne) The Haworth Press, Inc., 1998, pp. 69-83; and: *Living "Difference": Lesbian Perspectives on Work and Family Life* (ed: Gillian A. Dunne) Harrington Park Press, an imprint of The Haworth Press, Inc., 1998, pp. 69-83. Single or multiple copies of this article are available for a fee from The Haworth Document Delivery Service [1-800-342-9678, 9:00 a.m. - 5:00 p.m. (EST). E-mail address: getinfo@haworthpressinc.com].

69

is done for assumes key importance. The ways in which lesbians may or may not be constituted as 'housewives' are then unpacked and evaluated in terms of women's relationships to 'family' and in terms of 'housewife' as task-doer. Finally, a plea for the reclamation of the 'housewife,' and the associated need to place gender center-stage, is made evident. *[Article copies available for a fee from The Haworth Document Delivery Service: 1-800-342-9678. E-mail address: getinfo@haworthpressinc.com]*

INTRODUCTION

For some time now, feminist sociologists and others have been following reports from both North America and the UK of changes in the organization of family and household work in co-residing, heterosexual couple-based households (Benjamin and Sullivan 1996; Berk-Fenstermaker 1985; Brannen and Moss 1991; Goodnow and Bowes 1994; Gregson and Lowe 1993). Right-wing anxiety about changes in family life often centers upon the assumed loss of social cohesion represented by the breakdown of those roles and responsibilities thought to mark traditional gender divisions in family and household work (largely involving domestic labor, childcare, emotion work and kin-keeping activities undertaken within and between households). Moreover, households based upon the co-residing nuclear family are often idealized as natural and beneficial, contributing to fears that other kinds of household arrangements cannot adequately replace them. However, with the increasing visibility of households based around non-heterosexual relationships, sometimes but not always involving co-residing couples, the issue of how household work gets divided when there is, on the face of it, no 'housewife' present (or where everyone is one) becomes more complex. How do non-heterosexuals organize their family and household work? Given the attention which feminist sociologists have paid to the analysis of problems which beset women in heterosexual couple-based households (Delphy and Leonard 1992), the possibilities represented by analyses which center the organization of household work in lesbian households hold out much promise, not least because they are long overdue.

DOING THINGS DIFFERENTLY?

It has generally been argued that work in households based upon heterosexual couples is inevitably and persistently gendered, whilst work in households based upon non-heterosexual relationships is not gendered in any obvious or predictable way.[1] This means that lesbian and gay households are seen as much less likely to rely upon and replicate established practices when organizing their division of domestic labour, child-care, emotion work and kin-keeping activities. As a result, non-heterosexual households have been seen in some research as freer to 'experiment' with exotic/erotic 'alternatives' (Elliot 1986). Such approaches tend however to present non-heterosexual households as colorful, showcase specimens belonging to deviant sub-cultures. Some research tends on the other hand to 'normalize' non-heterosexual households (Desaulniers 1991; Peace 1993; Peplau and Cochran 1990), suggesting that household work in co-residing, lesbian couple households is largely based upon self-evident calculations and practicalities (involving such things as skills, abilities, preferences, energies, time schedules and physical limitations), with household work for the most part being perceived as equally shared, that is as being based upon 'mutual agreement over what constitutes a fair exchange' (Desaulniers 1991: 9).

What this 'normalizing' approach tends to do however is to empty non-heterosexual households of any processes and practices involving gendering. More specifically, gender *differences* are not thought to play any part in the organization of household work in lesbian (or gay) households. Although there was some evidence of specialism in Desaulniers' study, for example in cooking or laundry, nowhere did the same woman specialize in both, suggesting the absence of a single unitary 'housewife' amongst the lesbian couples interviewed. Similarly, Peace (1993) found that lesbians, unlike heterosexual women, felt the responsibility for housework was never theirs alone but was shared with other household members (women and children). Peace also found very little specialization, so that, for example, if one woman regularly repaired household equipment, she would not necessarily do other same-gender activities such as gardening or car maintenance. Finally, where tasks were found to consistently fall to one partner, Peace claims that they were undertaken on the grounds of 'time, ability and consideration' (Peace 1993: 30). However, these studies are limited in that although lesbian couple-based households are seen as distinct from heterosexual couple-based households in terms of being settings in which no men (as husbands or partners) are present, they mirror them in terms of taking co-residing coupledom as their focus. They then, by virtue of focusing upon the absence of men, denude lesbian households of any gendering processes whatsoever so that household work becomes constituted as egalitarian, by virtue of being shared on the basis of such things as skills, abilities, preferences and so on. Gendering, in the sense of doing gender difference, is simply erased in favour of an androgynous 'doing of togetherness.'

More recent British research on households which are organized around non-heterosexual relationships (Dunne 1997a, 1997b, 1998a, 1998b; Heaphy et al. 1997; Weeks et al. 1998) has argued for the benefits which accrue from what are seen as chosen, non-conventional modes of family and household organization. This recent research tends to present evidence that non-heterosexual households mark a radical departure from dominant heterosexual forms, and offer lesbians (and gay men) a unique potential for creating more democratic-egalitarian living arrangements, albeit involving considerable amounts of emotion work (Dunscombe and Marsden 1993) in the form of discussions of and negotiations around who does what, when, how and for whom (Heaphy et al. 1997). It is argued that there are fewer set patterns, expectations and assumptions in non-heterosexual households and greater possibilities for fashioning and inventing more democratic-egalitarian 'modes of relating.'[2] To an extent then lesbians (and gay men) are now seen as doing things not only differently from but also better than heterosexuals when it comes to the routine organization of family and household work within and between households.

Specifically and to some extent following from previous research, there are some indications in this more recent research that non-heterosexuals are able to 'de-gender' household work, thus (for lesbians in particular) denuding it of its oppressive aspects. For example, in the 'Families of Choice' project (Heaphy et al. 1997; Weeks et al. 1998), lesbian interviewees identified as especially problematic the ways in which heterosexual women were subject to specific cultural imperatives based around their gendered roles and responsibilities (as wives/mothers). This was seen to open up possibilities for lesbian couples in terms of not falling into dichotomized gender roles. As a result, inequalities based upon gender difference as constituted in lesbians' intimate, interpersonal relationships have been seen as (potentially at least) absent. As Dunne (1997a) argues: '(t)he analysis of lesbian partnerships is important because it provides visions of divisions of household and market labour which are not structured by dichotomous gender scripts' (p. 179).[3]

Furthermore, in more recent research, Dunne (1997b; 1998b) has found that this egalitarianism, based upon lesbians' occupation of a similar gender power base, extends to lesbians who parent (and co-parent) dependent children. Being a lesbian birth-mother of a young child in a same-sex cohabiting partnership, it is argued, is characterized by a number of criteria which mark lesbian parents out as different from heterosexual co-habiting parents. These criteria include more creative and balanced household work strategies, with same-sex partners both lowering their commitment (like mothers more generally) to their careers whilst their child(ren) are young, as well as experiencing a lack of access to gender-differentiated ideas about how each partner should enact her parenting, such that lesbian birth-mothers are unlikely to think of their partners simply as 'breadwinners' (Dunne 1997b). This has led Dunne to argue that linked to the capacity to evaluate and move beyond heterosexuality, is the crucial importance of developing broader theoretical conceptions of *womanhood*, of addressing the contention that we become different sorts of women when we are with women or men. Unlike some previous research, Dunne and I are pressing for the need to take gender fully into account; to acknowledge that in the work that lesbians do, we are constrained and empowered *as women*. This theme–of exploring the complex ways in which gender is still marked in and through situations of 'gender parity' as evidenced in lesbian partnerships–has also been central to Dunne's latest works (1998a; 1998b) and to my work on 'queer housewives' (Oerton 1997).

COMMONALITIES AND DIFFERENCES

So although emphasis is often placed upon the differences between heterosexuals and non-heterosexuals in terms of the ways in which household work is organized, I want to further develop the argument that for both lesbians and heterosexual women, there is a relational quality to the doing of gender (see Dunne 1998b). Lesbians do share many of the same responsibilities (and opportunities) that typically accrue to women generally for intra- and inter-household work (Finch 1989; Finch and Mason 1993; Malos 1995). In many respects lesbians share crucially in the experiences of heterosexual women since women generally are more likely than men to take responsibility for certain kinds of household work, especially that involving intimate care (Finch and Groves 1983). As daughters, mothers, nieces, aunts, sisters and friends, lesbians can be seen as engaging in similar relations, conditions and exchanges of household work as heterosexual women. In some respects, for example as never-married women, lesbians may be seen as *more* available to take up these positions within family/kin networks. Crucial to the organization of family and household work undertaken by both heterosexual and lesbian women, I would argue then, are deeply embedded *gendering processes and practices*, particularly as they pertain to relational exchanges of work undertaken within and between households, and kin/friendship networks, as built up over time.[4] But, as was argued in the previous section, there has been a tendency in some of the research on the organization of household work in non-heterosexual households to throw out gender as a contender in the theoretical playing field (Desaulniers 1991; Peace 1993). This, I would argue, is because gender has been conceived of as primarily operating in terms of gender *difference*, and furthermore, as gender difference operating for the most part in co-residing, couple-based relationships, so that gender difference becomes constituted primarily in terms of 'who we do gender for' (Dunne 1998b). I want to suggest however that it is in and through the specific locatedness of lesbians as gendered subjects positioned in complex relations in and between diverse households that the conditions and exchanges of household work undertaken by lesbians can be more comprehensively understood. In short, paying attention to gender is more useful than erasing it.

Weeks et al. (1998) also allude to this when they note that there was rarely much cross-over between lesbians and gay men in the non-heterosexual households and kin/friendship networks they studied; in short, what appears to characterize many lesbians is that they are located in all-women (and sometimes women-only) family, kin and community settings. In this lesbians may share much in common with heterosexual women for whom all-women kin/friendship networks are crucial arenas for the sharing of responsibilities for household work, particularly between households. However, the 'same-sex' aspects of lesbians' lives, which do allow for a focus upon the gendering processes informing lesbianism, with lesbians all positioned as 'women,' often get collapsed onto the 'same-sexuality' aspects of lesbians' lives, so that all lesbians are positioned, like gay men, as 'non-heterosexual.' As a result of these elisions, the commonalities and differences between lesbians and other (heterosexual) women and the commonalities and differences between lesbians and non-heterosexual men, are often inadequately specified. Consequently, there has been a tendency to argue, as stated earlier, that by virtue of being non-heterosexual, both lesbians and gay men escape the oppressive (gendered) aspects of household work. Power is seen as equally shared rather than accruing to a 'head of household,' for whom 'housewives' then work.

Clearly then, analysis of the relations and conditions under which family, kin and household work is performed by lesbians *as women*, is crucial for any specification of the commonalties and differences operating here. Arising from a self-reflexive analysis of my own domestic labor, child-care, emotion work and kin-keeping activities as undertaken in a single (typical) fortnight or so, it is possible to problematize the extent to which differences based around sexuality alone matter.[5] During that time, I dog- and cat-sat for, gave lifts to, shopped and cooked with my (non-co-residing) lesbian partner (of more than six years), played with the children of, gardened for and was fed by (and washed up for) several lesbian and heterosexual women friends. Additionally, I undertook numerous household tasks related to the up-keep of my own home (jointly owned for nearly ten years with my blood sister, and lived in by the two of us plus her six-year-old daughter) and supported and 'cared for' my elderly and frail parents, who live (semi-independently) less than five miles away. Some of this work was tiring and demanding, some of it was pleasurable and rewarding. However, it does not appear to me that the responsibilities I took for the household work I engaged in were so very radically different from the responsibilities for household work undertaken by my sister (a single heterosexual woman).[6] In terms of the relations under which such inter- and intra-household work was carried out, we are both 'daughters,' 'sisters,' 'aunts,' 'friends' and so forth to those that make up our immediate household and close kin/friendship networks.

Furthermore, neither of us are 'housewives' in the sense that we are not engaging in household work for (co-residing) male partners/ husbands. It might simply appear then that what constitutes the freedoms we as lesbians (or single heterosexual women) have to 'do our gender differently' (Dunne 1998b) when it comes to organizing our household work is that we are doing it largely if not solely for women, but not for men (and certainly not for men as husbands/ partners). But in and of itself this seems reductionist; can it simply be the case that what matters most is who the household work is done *for*? Does the absence of a (heterosexual) man (as partner/husband) erase all the processes and practices associated with gendering? Dunne (1998a) argues and illustrates that once the man is introduced, women are then incorporating men's share of domestic work within their area of responsibility. They thereby become housewives only in relation to men. But can lesbians, inasmuch as we too take responsibility for keeping the dust at bay and the food on the table, also be 'housewives'?

WHO IS A 'HOUSEWIFE'?

Whilst 'lesbian mothers' are no longer a contradiction in terms (Hanscombe 1982; Romans 1992; Saffron 1994), 'lesbian housewife' is clearly far more problematic. Does being a 'housewife' only become meaningful under heterosexual relations, such that lesbians can never be 'housewives'? It is often argued that the gender power relations involved in heterosexual housewifery traditionally constitute heterosexual women's relations with partners/ husbands as being in right wing rhetoric, natural and complementary, whilst being from feminist perspectives, oppressive. So, at the heart of the matter lies heterosexual women's relation to men as husbands/partners, and surely lesbians are free of all that? In short, lesbians cannot be housewives.

Some of the difficulties here, it seems to me, lie in the way that 'housewife' and 'housework' are imprecisely specified, often being conflated and separated as and when it suits political agendas. If 'housewife' is a unitary gendered and sexualized identity/social position/descriptive label which attaches to sexed bodies/sexual identities (heterosexual women's), it is not tenable for one lesbian-as-housewife to work for another because 'housewife' is here constituted in terms of pre-given, binary opposites predicated around a crucial difference, that of gendered heterosexuality. In the case of 'housewife' as a relation of power, lesbians cannot be housewives since this would necessarily involve undertaking household work for men as husbands/ partners. Men furthermore are absolutely precluded from being housewives themselves since they are the ones for whom household work is done, not the ones who do it.[7] So in this sense, 'lesbian housewife' is a contradiction in terms.

But if 'housewife' as task-doer inheres in housework itself, irrespective of who it is done for, then if a lesbian undertakes household 'duties,' she can be a 'housewife' (despite the absence of a male partner/husband) simply by virtue of undertaking housework itself. More specifically, the closer that work is to the traditionally gendered work undertaken by (heterosexual) women as housewife task-doers, the more appropriate it becomes to see whoever performs such work (and this may include some men, particularly non-heterosexual ones) as a 'housewife.' It also opens up the possibility that *both* women in co-residing lesbian couple-based households can be 'housewives.' Furthermore, if we deny that 'housewife' can inhere in the amount, type and extent of household work undertaken, then we are in danger of denying that lesbians' lives can be and often are marked by work that not only involves both day-to-day economic and emotional support and long-term projects such as life-long co-residency and child-rearing (Johnson 1990), but also in many respects mirrors the work that characterizes heterosexual women's lives. Lesbians do buy houses and furniture, make wills, take out insurance, cook, clean and raise children; in this they are not so very different from some of their heterosexual women counterparts.[8] In this way, it is not simply *who the work is done for* but *rather the doing of the work itself* that is centred for analysis; in this respect, like heterosexual women, lesbians can indeed be 'housewives.'

Furthermore, if 'housewife' as identity in the postmodern sense is dynamic, shifting and unstable (as all identities are), then both (or all) members of non-heterosexual households can be 'housewives' (or not as the case may be). It has been argued that what differences as are evident may lie in the notions of *choice* and *commitment* as differently constituted in lesbian households and kin/friendship networks vis-à-vis heterosexual ones (Dunne 1997a, 1997b; Weeks et al. 1998). Choices and commitments are often seen as fluid and negotiable, and as a result 'housewife' can be a highly contingent subject position to occupy and can attach at a number of different levels, in different historically specific and spatially-organized ways. 'Housewife' as subject position might potentially be taken up by any lesbian, albeit in ways which are socially and spatially marked. It is also possible that lesbians can parody the 'housewife' in similar ways to that claimed by lesbian 'brides' (and 'grooms'). Being a woman's 'kept woman' might even be seen as an attractive option and some lesbians I know have even made allusions to finding a 'sugar-mummy.' If we throw out the gendered housewife because she is enduringly subject to power relations based upon the doing of gender difference for men as husbands/partners (Dunne 1998b), we are in danger of losing sight of the diverse and complex ways in which gendering processes and practices might be operating in non-heterosexual households as well as losing sight of the importance of finding ways of marking the borders of what constitutes 'housewifery' in all its glorious complexity (Oerton 1997).

CONCLUSIONS

Women who are lesbians are likely to belong to communities in which the conscious constructedness of family, household and kin relations is more obviously manifest (Weston 1991).[9] Lesbians have been shown to create new ways of being, and to value democratic-egalitarian forms of relatedness (Weeks et al. 1998). However, there has been a tendency in some research on lesbians and household work to dismiss complex gendering processes and practices and to empty lesbians' lives (particularly when lived out in co-residing couple households) of any gendering dynamics, such that the doing of gender difference, and in particular the embeddedness of the construct '(heterosexual) woman-as-housewife,' gets analytically separated out as irrelevant to lesbians' lives.[10] In short, lesbians, it is thought, are not and cannot be seen as housewives because same-sex partners tend not to enact their work within the same relational matrices as heterosexual men and heterosexual women. In this article I have attempted to point to some of the limitations of such an approach. Perhaps it is now time for (some) lesbians to choose to reclaim the long-discredited and much maligned identity of 'housewife' as task-doer and to come out, alongside their heterosexual sisters, as visibly houseproud and care-giving women who routinely undertake important, challenging and demanding family, kin and household work. This might lead to strategies for political action which highlight the contention that virtually no woman escapes the processes and practices which constitute women (even lesbians) as having a *gendered* relationship to family and household work.

NOTES

1. Not all research upon household work in heterosexual couple households suggests that the gendering of household work follows fixed and immutable patterns, and indeed it would be surprising if it did. In recent research on anti-sexist (or 'less gendered') heterosexual couple households, there is some evidence of an emphasis on 'creating' relationships which do not conform to the dominant forms (Van Every 1995). Van Every's research shows that a critical awareness of anti-sexist values can reconfigure the organization of household work in such households in ways which can be seen as less oppressive of heterosexual women. However, Van Every also argues that one of the major limitations on the ability of such households to forge successful anti-sexist living arrangements is the reliance upon men's contribution: 'Men have chosen an egalitarian living arrangement but they can also change their minds. Thus anti-sexist living arrangements are only possible in so far as men are willing to live that way. Men are still heads of household but are using their power to allow a more equal division of labour' (Van Every 1995: 55).

2. This 'mode of relating' has been variously termed an 'egalitarian ideal' or 'friendship model' (Peplau et al. 1996), 'intimate friendship' (Dunne 1997a) or 'erotic friendship' (Blasius 1994). Nardi (1992) has referred to a model of 'friends as family' and Weeks et al. (1998) to 'elective families' and 'affinity circles,' all of which also capture the sense that non-heterosexual family and kin networks are not only chosen and created but also somehow more accepting, accommodating and satisfying spaces for lesbians and gay men to be.

3. Dunne (1997a) identifies three main styles of task organization in lesbian households which she terms the 'symmetric shared approach' in which household tasks are performed together or taken in turns, the 'symmetric specialized approach' in which household tasks are divided according to particular likes and dislikes, and the 'asymmetric approach' in which task allocation and execution are unequal (pp. 206-215). Although in some cases task allocation was asymmetric, most respondents in Dunne's study were found to have 'embraced an egalitarian approach to household labor' (pp. 214). This contrasts with the more gender polarized divisions of labour that traditionally mark heterosexual households.

4. Dunne (1997b) explored approaches to kinwork in her recent study and found that unlike the tendency in heterosexual couple-based households for women to take this on, each of the lesbian partners she interviewed retained responsibility for their own kin. Additionally, as yet no examples were found in her study of lesbian respondents doing domestic and child-care work for kin, although there were quite high levels of kin involvement in respondents' lives, for example, help with babysitting. However, I would suggest that lesbians do undertake various forms of kin work which could be seen to befall them as (non-married) women, such as care of elderly and infirm parents, young nephews and nieces, etc. Many lesbians also co-parent children with other women, and may not have a live-in relationship in order to do so. In addition, many lesbians engage in irregular tasks such as house- and pet-sitting, lift shares, decorating, renovation and gardening, shopping and cooking for both our 'blood' and 'chosen' kin and for friends. In times of difficulty, when relationships break down or when ill-health or bereavement strikes, lesbians often provide strong, solidaristic support networks for one another, and for other (heterosexual) women to whom we are close and committed. It is in these respects that lesbians may not be so dissimilar from heterosexual women, for whom reciprocity and mutuality amongst kin and other close 'community' (friends, neighbours) features as an important component of the organization and management of their everyday domestic lives (Finch 1989; Finch and Mason 1993). In short, whilst it is important to suggest that non-heterosexuals may be doing things differently, when it comes to specifying the gender dynamics operating here, the relations and conditions of work undertaken in lesbian households and kin networks may not be so very different from the relations and conditions of work undertaken by heterosexual women as we might think.

5. This self-reflexivity is encouraged and advocated in much lesbian-orientated theory and practice. Dunne (1997a) for example, argues '(i)t seems that women negotiating lesbian relationships have to engage in an unusual amount of

creativity, and this requires reflection upon and evaluation of what constitutes interpersonal relationships' (p. 184).

6. Interestingly, some surprising (and deeply embedded) gendering processes have occurred in the context of my position as one of two women living in a household with a small child, who has on several occasions insisted on positioning me in a dichotomized gender role relationship with her (biological) mother (my sister). In her pre-school years (aged between two and three or thereabouts), she variously referred to me as a 'man' (who in one case was ineligible to enter the 'ladies' toilets in a motorway service station), as her mother's 'husband,' and even at one stage as her (being herself at the time a four-year-old girl) 'boyfriend,' all of which concepts she employed with seemingly more aplomb than her later (aged between five and six) employment of the concept of 'aunt,' which she still only tends to apply to me at a public level and in the company of other (often newly acquired) child-friends.

7. What all this implies is that *only* women/wives can engage in personal and domestic servicing of other household members, and *only* men/husbands can indirectly 'help out' since a husband's contribution is necessarily assigned the status of a gift or favour to his domesticated wife. This also means that *only* men/husbands can be conceived of as relieving women/wives of household work, often taking on the tasks that are the most rewarding and high status (usually the ones that are also constituted as having flexible schedules and are the least repetitive) because the rump of the household work *has* to be her responsibility. She cannot therefore be in a position to help him with his housework, whilst he can help her with selected tasks as and when he chooses. Finally, because of these gendered power relations, child-care for fathers is often conceived of in terms of his 'playing' with children rather than 'caring' for them; for example, fathers are constituted as the ones who talk to or amuse the children until bedtime, while mothers are the ones occupied with clearing up the day's mess or getting the children's things ready for the next morning, since mothers can never just 'play' with their children.

8. In much of the contemporary writing on the politics of lesbian and gay experience however, the issue of household work is often seen as everyday, trivial and of little interest compared to other aspects of lesbians' lives. Some lesbians (and gay men) have perpetuated the idea that issues of how and when the household work gets done and by whom is boring. This is especially problematic given the ways in which lesbianism has been overtly sexualized such that what lesbians do in bed is thought to be more interesting than what we do when we shop, cook, clean or take our children to school.

9. As Van Every (1995) has noted, much existing research on family and household work is limited because of the inattention given to different means of reckoning 'kinship,' such that 'blood' relatives and those (potentially 'chosen' *and* 'blood' kin) to whom one has on-going commitments are elided. In Finch and Mason's (1993) research, for example, it remains unclear whether responsibilities accrue to household members because they are defined as kin, whether individuals become kin through taking on inter- and intra-household responsibilities, or

some combination of the two. The fact that the participants in Finch and Mason's study were defined as kin through 'blood' as well as the exchange of work makes this issue difficult to resolve.

10. This refusal or reluctance to be seen (or want to be seen) as 'housewives' amongst lesbians interviewed by Dunne (1997a) is evident in comments made by Angela: 'I am not a fanatical housewife' (p. 205), Nicola: 'I think the price might be [. . .] to, in fact, become the very kind of housewife that I have no wish to become' (p. 190) and Ruth: 'I certainly wouldn't want to fit into a wife role . . . ' (p. 210).

REFERENCES

Benjamin, O. and Sullivan, O. (1996) 'The importance of difference: conceptualising increased flexibility in gender relations at home' in *Sociological Review* 44 (2): 225-251.

Berk-Fenstermaker, S. (1985) *The Gender Factory: The Apportionment of Work in American Households* New York: Plenum Press.

Blasius, M. (1994) *Gay and Lesbian Politics: Sexuality and the Emergence of a New Ethic* Philadelphia: Temple University Press.

Brannen, J. and Moss, P. (1991) *Managing Mothers; Dual Earner Households After Maternity Leave* London: Unwin Hyman.

Delphy, C. and Leonard, D. (1992) *Familiar Exploitation: A New Analysis of Marriage in Contemporary Western Society* Cambridge: Polity Press in association with Blackwell.

Desaulniers, S. (1991) 'The Organization of Housework in Lesbian Households,' Paper presented at the Canadian Women's Studies Association Learned Societies, Queen's University, Kingston, July 29th-31st 1991.

Dunne, G. A. (1997a) *Lesbian Lifestyles: Women's Work and the Politics of Sexuality* London: Macmillan.

Dunne, G. A. (1997b) *'Why Can't A Man Be More Like A Woman?: In Search of Balanced Domestic and Employment Lives'* LSE Gender Institute Discussion Paper Series, 3, March 1997.

Dunne, G. A. (1998a) ' "Pioneers Behind Our Own Front Doors": New Models for the Organization of Work in Partnerships' in *Work, Employment and Society*, March 1988.

Dunne, G. A. (1998b) 'A Passion For 'Sameness'?: Sexuality and Gender Accountability' in Smart, C. and Silva, E. (eds.) (1998) *The New Family?* London: Sage.

Dunscombe, J. and Marsden, D. (1993) 'Love and Intimacy: The Gender Division of Emotion and Emotion Work' in *Sociology* 27 (2): 221-241.

Elliot, F.R. (1986) *The Family; Change or Continuity?* Houndmills, Basingstoke: Macmillan.

Finch, J. (1989) *Family Obligations and Social Change* Cambridge: Polity.

Finch, J. and Groves, D. (1983) *A Labour of Love: Women, Work and Caring* London: Routledge and Kegan Paul.

Finch, J. and Mason, J. (1993) *Negotiating Family Responsibilities* London: Routledge.

Goodnow, J. J. and Bowes, J. M. (1994) *Men, Women and Household Work* Oxford, Oxford University Press.

Gregson, N. and Lowe, M. (1993) 'Renegotiating The Domestic Division of Labour? A Study of Dual Career Households in North East and South East England' in *Sociological Review,* 41: 475-505.

Hanscombe, G.E. (1982) *Rocking The Cradle: Lesbian Mothers, A Challenge in Family Living* London: Sheba.

Heaphy, B., Donovan, C. and Weeks, J. (1997) 'Sex, Money and the Kitchen Sink: Power in Same Sex Couple Relationships' Paper presented to the British Sociological Association Annual Conference, 'Power/Resistance,' University of York, April 1997.

Johnson, S. (1990) *Staying Power: Long Term Lesbian Couples* Tallahassee, Florida: The Naiad Press.

Malos, E. (1980, rev ed. 1995) *The Politics of Housework* Cheltenham: New Clarion Press.

Nardi, P. (1992) 'That's What Friends Are For: Friends As Family in the Gay and Lesbian Community' in Plummer, K. (ed.) (1992) *Modern Homosexualities: Fragments of Lesbian and Gay Experience* London: Routledge.

Oerton, S. (1997) 'Queer Housewives?': Some Problems in Theorizing the Division of Domestic Labour in Lesbian and Gay Partnerships/Households in *Women's Studies International Forum, Special Issue: Concepts of Home* (20) 3, May-June 1997.

Peace, H.F. (1993) 'The Pretended Family–A Study of the Division of Domestic Labour in Lesbian Families' Leicester University Discussion Papers in Sociology, No. S93/3.

Peplau, L.A. and Cochran, S.D. (1990) 'A Relationship Perspective in Homosexuality' in McWhirter, D., Sanders, D.D. and Reinisch, J.M. (eds.) *Homosexuality/ Heterosexuality: Concepts of Sexuality* Oxford, Oxford University Press.

Peplau, L.A., Venigas, R.C. and Miller Campbell, S. (1996) 'Gay and Lesbian Relationships' in Savin-Williams, R.C. and Cohen, K.M. (eds.) *The Lives of Lesbians, Gays and Bisexuals* New York: Harcourt Brace College.

Romans, P. (1992) 'Daring To Pretend? Motherhood and Lesbianism' in Plummer, K. (ed.) (1992) *Modern Homosexualities: Fragments of Lesbian and Gay Experience* London: Routledge.

Saffron, L. (1994) *Challenging Conceptions: Pregnancy and Parenting Beyond the Traditional Family* London and New York: Cassell.

Van Every, J. (1995) *Heterosexual Women Changing the Family: Refusing to be a 'Wife!'* London: Taylor and Francis.

Weeks, J., Donovan, C. and Heaphy, B. (1998) 'Everyday Experiments: Narratives of Non-Heterosexual Relationships' in Silva, E. and Smart, C. (1998) (eds.) *The New Family?* London: Sage.

Weston, K. (1991) *Families We Choose: Lesbians, Gays, Kinship* New York: Columbia University Press.

Working Out:
Lesbian Teachers and the Politics
of (Dis)Location

Gill Clarke

SUMMARY. This paper explores the significance of space(s) for the construction and contestation of lesbian teachers' sexual identities. In so doing it reveals how spaces are not neutral, but are shot through with power, such that some locations, be they public or private, become hostile places for lesbians. Nevertheless, queer activists have begun to reclaim the largely heterosexual landscape and to extend the boundaries of sexual citizenship. Schools in England however remain largely sites of compulsory heterosexuality, where few have dared to cross the (sexual) boundaries. Finally, attention is also directed to the city and to

Gill Clarke lectures in physical education and biographical studies at the University of Southampton. Prior to this she was field leader for physical education at Chichester Institute of Higher Education after having taught in secondary schools in Hampshire. She is an officer of the British Sociological Association Study Group on Auto/Biography and on the editorial boards of *The Journal of Sport Pedagogy* and the *European Journal of Physical Education*. She has co-edited *Researching Women and Sport* (Macmillan) and published articles on lesbian physical education students and teachers.

Address correspondence to Gill Clarke, University of Southampton, Research and Graduate School of Education, Highfield, Southampton, England, SO17 1BJ (e-mail: gmc@soton.ac.uk).

The author is grateful to the editor Dr. Gillian Dunne, Dr. Sarah Gilroy and Professor Sheila Scraton for their helpful comments on an earlier version of this paper.

[Haworth co-indexing entry note]: "Working Out: Lesbian Teachers and the Politics of (Dis)Location." Clarke, Gill. Co-published simultaneously in *Journal of Lesbian Studies* (The Haworth Press, Inc.) Vol. 2, No. 4, 1998, pp. 85-99; and: *Living "Difference": Lesbian Perspectives on Work and Family Life* (ed: Gillian A. Dunne) The Haworth Press, Inc., 1998, pp. 85-99; and: *Living "Difference": Lesbian Perspectives on Work and Family Life* (ed: Gillian A. Dunne) Harrington Park Press, an imprint of The Haworth Press, Inc., 1998, pp. 85-99. Single or multiple copies of this article are available for a fee from The Haworth Document Delivery Service [1-800-342-9678, 9:00 a.m. - 5:00 p.m. (EST). E-mail address: getinfo@haworthpressinc.com].

85

the home as sites of resistance and places for possible border crossings. *[Article copies available for a fee from The Haworth Document Delivery Service: 1-800-342-9678. E-mail address: getinfo@haworthpressinc.com]*

INTRODUCTION

(Work) spaces are neither pure nor innocent, for not only are they gendered, but they are also racialized, sexed and (hetero)sexualized. As Bell and Valentine (1995:8) comment, 'A whole body of work is emerging in geography that explores the performance of sexual identities and the way that they are inscribed on the body and the landscape.' With few exceptions (see Bensimon, 1992; Prendergast and Forrest, 1997; Shilling, 1991; Sparkes, 1996; Thorne, 1993) this approach has yet to extend into the educative context in general and physical education specifically.[1] The ensuing analysis seeks to begin to redress this by revealing the significance that space has for the contestation, construction, and constraining of lesbian physical education teachers' sexual identities in England. As Shilling (1991:23) states, 'Space is no longer seen merely as an environment in which interaction takes place, but is itself deeply implicated in the production of individual identities and social inequalities.' Furthermore, it is clearly also an environment where relations of power (and powerlessness), privilege, domination and social control are established.

In seeking to illustrate these claims I draw on qualitative data generated from my research with eighteen lesbian physical education teachers who were white, able-bodied and aged between 23 and 47. Some were single, some had been married, some were currently in long-standing lesbian relationships, none had children. They had been teaching for just over one year to twenty-five years. All taught pupils aged between 11-18, some worked in mixed state schools, others in girls' schools, church schools or private schools located in inner cities, urban or rural areas. In order to conceptualize how they live out their lesbianism it is essential to understand how the state has sought to regulate sexuality through the passing of Section 28 of the Local Government Act in England and Wales in 1988.[2] It stated:

1. A local authority shall not–
   a. intentionally promote homosexuality or publish material with the intention of promoting homosexuality;

b. promote the teaching in any maintained school of the acceptability of homosexuality as a pretended family relationship.

2. Nothing in subsection (1) above shall be taken to prohibit the doing of anything for the purpose of treating or preventing the spread of disease.

This legislation was arguably designed to maintain cultural (and spatial) conformity whilst at the same time defining, regulating, policing, and enforcing sexual boundaries. Although this law has been summarily dismissed as ambiguously worded and has yet to be interpreted by the courts, it has created symbolic borders which few lesbian teachers have dared to openly cross. Furthermore, it has had a major impact on the lives of lesbian and gay teachers causing many of them to fear for the continuation of their employment should their sexuality be revealed.

In connection with the aforementioned claims about space it is necessary to explain how I conceptualize 'space.' Thus I write not as a geographer but as a lesbian feminist educator who is interested in how the notion of space impacts on (and for some of us defines) our sexual identities and how subsequently we come to express ourselves and the places we 'choose' (or are permitted) to visit and/or inhabit. For me, space is not static, rather it is dynamic, fluid and liable to destabilize in the face of queer challenges (see Ingram et al., 1997). So, whilst space (and places) may influence and shape who we are, we too can (and do) act back on space such that the spaces for sexual citizenship can be redrawn and enlarged. Space is not neutral, it is, as Bell et al. (1994:32) claim, 'socially and culturally encoded.' I would add also that space is temporally and historically produced. Consequently space is more than mere terrain, it is, as Blunt and Rose (1994:5) state, 'constituted through struggles over power/knowledge.' Hence, we need to ask what sort of territory do we have (and want), who controls it and more importantly who has access to it? What does the (sexual) landscape look like, what could it become?

PUBLIC AND (PARTIALLY) PRIVATE SPACES

In trying to answer these questions it is important to consider the concepts of public and private space since these have a powerful

and regulatory impact on the lives of many lesbian teachers in
England. Feminists have done much to destabilize the representa-
tion of the public/private as a dichotomy and to reveal how it is
'rooted in patriarchy' (Bensimon, 1992:99). They have also demonstrated how this artificial split works to conceal and preserve
women's domestic and economic exploitation and other realities of
their lives. Nevertheless, there is still much that we need to know
about how (hetero)sexual boundaries are established and how the
public has traditionally come to be associated with 'masculine'
(professional) activities and the private to be associated with 'feminine' (personal) activities. Moreover, it is evident that 'the association of sexuality with the private as distinct from the public sphere
is institutionalised' (Richardson, 1996:14). Hence, for instance, the
establishment of British laws around public order and decency
which work to enshrine the legitimacy and omnipotence of heterosexuality. Whilst on the surface it may appear that there is some
degree of tolerance for sexual minorities it is clear that what 'we' do
in the private sphere is 'acceptable' and tolerated only so long as we
do not step over the boundaries into the public domain. In effect
what this pseudo-liberal tolerance is saying is be a 'good homosexual' but don't be a 'dangerous queer' (Smith, 1997:221). In
other words know your (limited) sexual space, know when (and
where) you can come out of the closet, but equally make sure you
know when to climb (swiftly) back in.

These spatial binaries lead not only to the maintaining of hege-
monic heterosexual ideologies but also to deafening silences about
sexual oppression, and contribute to the belief that there is no problem here.[3] Despite the drawbacks of these public/private distinctions, I use them, albeit cautiously, for these issues must continue to
be in the public domain, for if they remain private issues it is
inevitable that the oppression of many women will continue to be
obscured and invisible to many. Furthermore, when these marginal
groups try to assert their rightful, democratic place on the landscape
they 'remain vulnerable to claims that they are trying to push into
the public realm unacceptable sexual practices' (Cooper, 1995:69).

Bensimon (1992:99) sees this public/private distinction as being
not only partial, but also distorting since sexuality becomes normal-
ized as heterosexuality; she contends that such a distinction is per-

verse because it 'provides a justification for not bringing about change.' This public/private distinction operates to universalize and sanction heterosexuality thereby maintaining the 'invisibility' of lesbians and 'others.'

However, it is important to note that not all private space is private; for some sexual minorities their 'private' sexual practices have been deemed criminal and illegal. This was evidenced recently by a British legal case (known as 'Operation Spanner' after the police code name) when a group of gay men who had engaged in consensual SM activities were convicted and imprisoned in December 1990 for a number of offenses including assault occasioning actual bodily harm (see Diva, April 1997). The judge's ruling was challenged but the appeals were quashed in February 1992. The men took their case to the European Court of Human Rights 'on the basis that there had been an unjustifiable interference with their right to a private life contrary to Article 8 of the European Convention on Human Rights' (Gay Times, April 1997:18). In 'a landmark ruling, the Strasbourg judges said that the Government had the right to interfere in the private lives of people to protect public health and morals' (Guardian, 2 February 1997). What this case demonstrates is the power and authority of the state to (re)draw and police the boundaries of sexual citizenship which hitherto have been private pleasure places (see Bell, 1995). Such moral patrolling raises fundamental questions about the ownership of bodies, sexual politics and the sanctity of private spaces. For some lesbians (and gays) there may be no utopias, be they private or public. This court ruling makes it clear that it is possible to be lesbian or gay only in specific places and spaces and that only certain forms of behaviour are legally approved (see Bristow, 1989).

Queer activists have begun to fight back through direct (in your face) action and through the formation of such oppositional groups as OutRage in London and Queer Nation in New York. These and other groups have staged various challenges to the assumed heterosexuality of places, as well as challenging:

the public-private split as a foundation for sexual citizenship, perhaps most notably through campaigns of 'outing' celebrities. . . . By refusing the rich and the famous the privacy once lobbied for by gay rights campaigns, queer activists have called into question the usefulness of the categories public and private by pushing, like AIDS activism, at the limits of both private and public spaces of sexual citizenship. (Bell, 1995:143)

Spatial pushes in London have included, for instance, a mass KISS-IN in Piccadilly Circus and a Queer Wedding in Trafalgar Square, both of which were organized by OutRage.

THE EDUCATIONAL LANDSCAPE AND WORKING SPACES

Due to the conservative nature of education and the power of the new moral right, together with the climate of fear that largely surrounds lesbian and gay teachers, few if any would dare to participate in such direct actions for fear of losing their teaching posts should their sexuality become public knowledge (see Clarke, 1996). For these lesbian teachers, being queer is not part of their lifestyles, indeed for some such public displays were viewed with dismay. Ethel,[4] for example, divulged how she thought '(they) give the general public a very poor example of what homosexuality is all about.'

In considering queer public displays only two of the lesbian teachers had been on the very visible Lesbian and Gay Pride march through London (the biggest lesbian and gay festival in Europe which annually attracts over 160,000 participants). Despite the potential safety and anonymity of such a large crowd one of the teachers who had attended described how she tried not to get too close to the edges of the march for fear of being seen and recognized by pupils or parents. These fears mean that many lesbian teachers rarely leave any public marks on the landscape. Invisibility for these lesbian teachers within the educative system becomes a way of negotiating and surviving the often hostile environment within which they work. For them the public/private split continues to be a daily reality as they largely conceal their lesbianism from teaching colleagues and pupils alike.

The strategies British lesbian teachers employ to conceal their identities are not too dissimilar to those employed by lesbian teachers in North America whereby they seek to pass as heterosexual (see Griffin, 1992; Khayatt, 1992; Woods, 1992). In so doing they engage in what might be described as the performance of (hetero-sexual) sexual identity; in conceptualising these 'acts' as perfor-mances I draw selectively on Butler's (1990, 1991, 1993) concept of gender performativity. This notion of performance provides a useful metaphor to play with since schools are rather like theatres where all sorts of performances are engaged in. Given the coercive power of heterosexuality the script for sexual identity is an espe-cially narrow and delimited one which requires the performers, be they front or back stage, to portray a particular part, that is 'the happy heterosexual.'

Inasmuch as I am claiming that heterosexuality is being played at I would not want to dispute that these women are not 'really' lesbian or that being a lesbian is something that you slip into and out of like some sort of sexual tourist. Rather it is that the nature of schooling and the socio-political context requires that they learn their heterosexual parts convincingly so as to be able to repeat them as and when required. Additionally, their lines are severely constrained (even compulsory) if their performances are to be socially sanctioned and publicly approved. Whilst this notion of performance provides crucial insights into the public ways that lesbian lives are largely lived out in schools it would be a gross mistake to fail to recognise that for these teachers they *have* to perform in order to survive in a homophobic and heterosexist world, therefore it is important not to trivialise these performances. The costs and risks for them should they not play their part are all too real and too painful to be denied. Their lives are more than a game (Clarke, 1997). Furthermore, as Esterberg comments:

> lesbian performances are serious play; that is, while there is an element of play, of fun, in the slippage of categories, this is serious play because it has to do with deeply important aspects of the self. Lesbian identity–and our playing out of it–*matters*. (1996:261)

Performing a particular part can, I would argue, be a subversive and resistant act, insofar as the performance is a way of throwing heterosexuality back in your face! Where the part is successfully performed then the point is made (albeit largely privately) that heterosexuality can be copied, faked and bought without it being realised that it is merely an imitation.

SEXUAL OUTLAWS AND CITY LIMITS

Perhaps in terms of safe spaces/places for the display of lesbian identities the 'city' (see Grosz, 1995) offers some vestige of hope, insofar as it may provide some degree of anonymity and freedom from the gaze of heterosexual others (be they parents, pupils, other teachers). But does this offer 'real' opportunities to develop and feel a sense of belonging (see Probyn, 1996), or is a situation created where an individual is at once inside and outside of the sexual mainstream? For some of these teachers the city did provide a sense of freedom and 'a bolt hole.' For Ivy it meant that she could go to lesbian meetings and gay pubs, for Deb she could go clubbing 'and be relaxed . . . (and) be myself.' However, others feared that when they went to clubs they might meet pupils or be seen by them when they left, hence most avoided going. Caroline recalled how when she went to a club in the city where she worked:

> the police intimidate you, I've been frightened to death of being arrested . . . they go along in their 'meat vans' (police vehicles) and they crawl along the edge of the curb as you walk and shout things at you.

For Caroline the city was not a safe place to be, for her and others it may be too hostile a terrain to visit and/or safely negotiate. A national survey by Stonewall (1996:7) of homophobic violence revealed how the 'majority of the attacks reported were in the vicinity of gay venues' and how 'One in three gay men responding (34%) and one in four women (24%) had experienced violence in the last five years because of their sexuality.'

The importance of where lives are lived and located should not be underestimated. The home should be a place to be yourself and a site that is free from the surveillance of others. This freedom, however, may not always be extended to those in the teaching profession (and in particular lesbian teachers). For the lesbian teachers in my research the home was not always a place where they could be themselves or a place of sanctuary. Most worried about living close to the school where they taught for fear of their pupils 'seeing things . . . and being watched all the time' (Annie). Lucy described how she preferred

> to live out of town and away from the immediate school envi-ronment . . . to protect whatever privacy I have left. It's still not total because my next door neighbour is a local shop owner in the school catchment area, what he doesn't know isn't worth knowing.

Barbara also felt strongly about where she located her private life; she stated:

> I would never live very close to my school, because . . . (of) the experience of my girlfriend who has had a lot of trouble and you have to hide what you are doing . . .

Her girlfriend Caroline, who she lived with and who was also a physical education teacher, had had the terrifying experience of having the windows in her car smashed by a gang of local 'lads.' Caroline described how

> this terrorizing all sort of came with dyke and lezzie PE teacher and I thought these people hate me and for nothing more than my sexuality or my job . . .

These accounts illustrate the complexity and paradoxical nature of the public/private split. The notion that private space is private clearly does not hold for many of the women in my research. Thus some are left dislocated from even their homes. Furthermore whilst they were in school they also often felt anxious when they were asked by pupils where they lived and who they lived with. Such questions were generally steered to safer topics or answered some-what ambiguously so as to deflect suspicion.

Heterosexual teachers may also want to avoid living in the immediate environment of their work places and they too may not wish to answer questions about their private lives. However, I would maintain that there are differences in how heterosexuality and homosexuality are viewed and valued. In seeking to support this contention Fuss's work is pertinent since she notes that heterosexuality 'typically defines itself in critical opposition to that which it is not: homosexuality' (1991:1). As such, homosexuality is both defined and constructed as a stigmatised, abnormal and marginal identity that is socially threatening. Like other dualisms these sexual discourses promote (and regulate) a hierarchical order where one of the terms is privileged over the other which is repressed and constrained, and here in the case of the dialectic of sexuality it is heterosexuality that takes on the privileged, omnipotent position.

In conceptualising these issues I have found Memmi's (1965) explanation of the colonial relationship and situation in 'The colonizer and the colonized' helpful as it provides a tool for understanding the relationship between heterosexuality and homosexuality. Memmi, a colonized Tunisian, shows how the colonizer constructs the colonized as marginal other and as lacking everything that the colonizer is. Thus it becomes possible to envisage parallels with the construction of heterosexuality, insofar as homosexuality also gets constructed as marginal other, as outsider and as stranger and is attributed negative qualities. It is also apparent that homosexuals are often portrayed as lacking the positive qualities that are attributed to heterosexuals and for lesbian teachers who work within the domain of physical education the situation is compounded for a number of reasons. These include the subject matter of physical education, that is the centrality and the physicality of the body, which creates additional anxieties, fears and pressures for these teachers. As Woods explains:

> In a society where homosexuals are stereotyped as child molesters who recruit young children to their so-called deviant lifestyles, female physical educators and coaches are prime targets for homophobic suspicions and accusations. (1992:92)

Although teachers of other subjects may be forced to deny their sexual identities what I am arguing for is the need to recognize that the gendered bodily culture of physical education creates a unique context for denial that might not be experienced by teachers within other subject disciplines. Furthermore, it should be recognised that physical education developed around two distinct and separate male and female sporting cultures built around particularly narrow ideologies and stereotyped visions of heterosexual masculinity and femininity. Thus within the male domain of sport and physical education the heterosexuality of women participants has often been open to question, for success in sport meant that perhaps they were not 'real' women and therefore lesbian. To be a lesbian in such an arena is to run the risk of harassment and intimidation (see Clarke, 1995; Lenskyj, 1991).

SPACES FOR BORDER CROSSINGS

At the beginning of this paper I asked what sort of territory we have. It is clear from this discussion that the terrain is no smooth landscape; rather it is pitted and hideously scarred by a sexual hegemony that erects borders to maintain (and protect) the sanctity and normalcy of heterosexuality. Globally it is apparent that borders are unstable, but for every border that is scaled or dismantled it seems that yet another is erected in its place.[5] Borders necessitate crossing and negotiation; for some sexual migrants this a matter of ease, but for those on the margins the 'right' identification papers may be missing, thus the borders that constitute sexual identity may unite or simultaneously divide. As Anzaldua incisively notes,

> Borders are set up to define the places that are safe and unsafe, to distinguish us from them. A border is a dividing line, a narrow strip along a steep edge. A borderland is a vague and undetermined place created by the emotional residue of an unnatural boundary. . . . The prohibited and forbidden are its inhabitants. Los atravesados live here: the squint-eyed, the perverse, the queer, the troublesome, the mongrel, the mulatto, the half-breed, the half-dead; in short, those who cross over, pass over, or go through the confines of the 'normal.' The only 'legitimate' inhabitants are those in power, the whites and those who align themselves with whites. Tension grips the inhabitants of the borderlands like a virus. (1987:3)

For those of us who cross over borders the experience may not be a comfortable one. We have much to learn from those whose lives have been colonised, oppressed, exploited and subjected to imperialism. hooks (1984:ix) in writing of her location on the margins and of black Americans comments 'We could enter that world but we could not live there. We had always to return to the margin. . . . ' hooks (1991) also reminds us that the margins can be sites of both resistance as well as repression, and I would add sites of transformation. For these lesbian teachers this is no easy task given their invisibility and isolation within schools. This lack of collective identity is also potentially problematic for their working together to create social and political change.

CONCLUDING REMARKS

The spaces to be a lesbian (physical education) teacher are severely restricted and contained; for these women their safe spaces are largely confined to the margins. Although their experiences may not be representative of other lesbian women they vividly illustrate how heterosexual spaces have to be negotiated and successfully 'passed' through if harassment and abuse are to be avoided. Their experiences demonstrate that their sexual identity 'choices' are severely constrained by a complexity of forces that operate within both the wider social and political world and the microcosm of the school. Thus whilst they 'make their own identities, . . . they do not make them just as they please' (Epstein, 1993-4:30). Inasmuch as I have employed Butler's notion of performance to convey how these lesbian teachers play a heterosexual part I do so with care. As Jeffreys (1994a, 1994b) comments, Butler's work on performance is based largely on gay male practices. Furthermore to view identity as simply a performance is dangerous as it could create a situation whereby the oppression of women by men is lost sight of. Additionally this concept of performance suggests that identity is freely chosen, but as we have seen there is nothing voluntary about the way that these teachers perform their heterosexual parts in the schooling context.

Finally, if spaces shape our sense of self and our sense of self shapes our spaces then until the sexual boundaries come tumbling down we will continue to be denied 'a place on the map . . . (and) also a place in history' (Rich, 1986:212).

NOTES

1. This is not to deny the important work in women's studies/philosophy/cultural studies of the likes of Grosz, Probyn and Butler on space, performance and identity.

2. It seems that the new Labour government will at some stage repeal it.

3. See Gaine's (1987, 1995) work re race and schooling, which is titled 'No problem here,' and the revised version: 'Still no problem here.'

4. All names are pseudonyms chosen by the women.

5. The charity War on Want (1997) published a report on 'Pride world-wide: sexuality, development and human rights' which highlights the rights of lesbians and gay men and how these are being abused in many developing countries.

REFERENCES

Anzaldua, Gloria (1987) *Borderlands: the New Mestiza = La Frontera.* San Francisco: Aunt Lute Book Company.

Bell, David (1995) 'Pleasure and danger: the paradoxical spaces of sexual citizenship,' *Political Geography,* 14, (2): 139-53.

Bell, David; Binnie, Jon; Cream, Julia and Valentine, Gill (1994) 'All hyped up and no place to go,' *Gender, Place and Culture,* 1, (1): 31-47.

Bell, David and Valentine, Gill (eds) (1995) *Mapping Desire: Geographies of Sexualities.* London: Routledge.

Bensimon, Estela Mara (1992) 'Lesbian existence and the challenge to normative constructions of the academy,' *Journal of Education,* 174, (3): 98-113.

Blunt, Alison and Rose, Gillian (eds) (1994) *Writing Women and Space: Colonial and Postcolonial Geographies.* London: The Guildford Press.

Bristow, Joseph (1989) 'Being gay: politics, identity, pleasure,' *New Formations,* 9, pp. 61-68.

Butler, Judith (1990) *Gender Trouble: Feminism and the Subversion of Identity.* London: Routledge.

Butler, Judith (1991) 'Imitation and gender insubordination' in D. Fuss (ed.), *Inside/Out Lesbian Theories, Gay Theories.* London: Routledge. pp. 13-31.

Butler, Judith (1993) *Bodies that Matter: on the Limits of 'Sex'.* London: Routledge.

Clarke, Gill (1995) 'Outlaws in sport and education? Exploring the sporting and education experiences of lesbian physical education teachers' in L. Lawrence, E. Murdoch and S. Parker (eds) *Professional and Development Issues in Leisure, Sport and Education.* Eastbourne: Leisure Studies Association. pp. 45-58.

Clarke, Gill (1996) 'Conforming and contesting with (a) difference: how lesbian students and teachers manage their identities,' *International Studies in Sociology of Education,* 6, (2): 191-209.

Clarke, Gill (1997) 'Playing a part: the lives of lesbian physical education teachers' in G. Clarke and B. Humberstone (eds) *Researching Women and Sport*. London: Macmillan. pp. 36-49.

Cooper, Davina (1995) *Power in Struggle: Feminism, Sexuality and the State*. Buckingham: Open University Press.

Diva (1997) *Spanner Case Ends in Defeat*. April, p. 17.

Epstein, Steven. (1996) 'A queer encounter: sociology and the study of sexuality' in S. Seidman (ed.), *Queer Theory/Sociology*. Oxford: Blackwell Publishers Ltd. pp. 145-67.

Esterberg, Kristin G. (1996) '"A certain swagger when I walk": performing lesbian identity' in S. Seidman (ed.), *Queer Theory/Sociology*. Oxford: Blackwell Publishers Ltd. pp. 259-79.

Fuss, Diana (1991) 'Inside/out' in D. Fuss (ed.), *Inside/Out Lesbian Theories, Gay Theories*. London: Routledge. pp. 1-10.

Gaine, Chris (1987) *No Problem Here: A Practical Approach to Education and Race in White Schools*. London: Hutchinson.

Gaine, Chris (1995) *Still No Problem Here*. Stoke on Trent: Trentham.

Gay Times (1997) *Spanner Case Ends in Defeat*. April, p. 19.

Griffin, Pat (1992) 'Identity management strategies among lesbian and gay educators,' *Qualitative Studies in Education*, 4, (3): 189-202.

Grosz, Elizabeth (1995) *Space, Time, and Perversion: Essays on the Politics of Bodies*. London: Routledge.

Guardian (1997) 2 February.

hooks, bell (1984) *Feminist Theory from Margin to Center*. Boston: South End Press.

hooks, bell (1991) *Yearning: Race, Gender and Cultural Politics*. London: Turnaround.

Ingram, Gordon Brent; Bouthillette, Anne-Marie and Retter, Yolanda (eds) (1997) *Queers in Space: Communities/Public Spaces/Sites of Resistance*. Seattle: Bay Press.

Jeffreys, Sheila (1994a) *The Lesbian Heresy: A Feminist Perspective on the Lesbian Sexual Revolution*. London: The Women's Press.

Jeffreys, Sheila (1994b) 'The queer disappearance of lesbians: sexuality in the academy,' *Women's Studies International Forum*, 17, (5) pp. 459-72.

Khayatt, Madiha Didi (1992) *Lesbian Teachers: an Invisible Presence*. New York: State University of New York Press.

Lenskyj, Helen (1991) 'Combating homophobia in sport and physical education,' *Sociology of Sport Journal*, 8, pp. 61-9.

Memmi, Albert (1965) *The Colonizer and the Colonized*. Boston: Beacon Press.

Prendergast, Shirley and Forrest, Simon (1997) ' "Hieroglyphs of the heterosexual": learning about gender in school' in L. Segal (ed.), *New Sexual Agendas*. London: Macmillan. pp. 180-95.

Probyn, Elspeth (1996) *Outside Belongings*. London: Routledge.

Rich, Adrienne (1986) *Blood, Bread, and Poetry: Selected Prose 1979-1985*. New York: W.W. Norton.

Richardson, Diane (ed.), (1996) *Theorising Heterosexuality: Telling it Straight.* Buckingham: Open University Press.

Shilling, Chris (1991) 'Social space, gender inequalities and educational differentiation,' *British Journal of Sociology of Education*, 12, (1): 23-44.

Smith, Anna Marie (1997) 'The good homosexual and the dangerous queer: resisting the "new homophobia"' in L. Segal (ed.), *New Sexual Agendas.* London: Macmillan. pp. 214-31.

Sparkes, Andrew (1996) 'Physical education teachers and the search for self: two cases of structured denial' in N. Armstrong (ed.), *New Directions in Physical Education: Change and Innovation.* London: Cassell. pp. 157-78.

Stonewall (1996) *Queer Bashing: A National Survey of Hate Crimes Against Lesbians and Gay Men.* London: Stonewall.

Thorne, Barrie (1993) *Gender Play.* Buckingham: Open University Press.

War on Want (1997) *Pride World-Wide: Sexuality, Development and Human Rights.* London: War on Want and Unison.

Woods, S. (1992) 'Describing the experiences of lesbian physical educators: a phenomenological study' in A.C. Sparkes (ed.), *Research in Physical Education and Sport: Exploring Alternative Visions.* London: The Falmer Press. pp. 90-117.

Index

Note: Page numbers followed by f indicate figures.

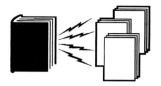

Haworth
DOCUMENT DELIVERY
SERVICE

This valuable service provides a single-article order form for any article from a Haworth journal.

- *Time Saving:* No running around from library to library to find a specific article.
- *Cost Effective:* All costs are kept down to a minimum.
- *Fast Delivery:* Choose from several options, including same-day FAX.
- *No Copyright Hassles:* You will be supplied by the original publisher.
- *Easy Payment:* Choose from several easy payment methods.

Open Accounts Welcome for . . .
- Library Interlibrary Loan Departments
- Library Network/Consortia Wishing to Provide Single-Article Services
- Indexing/Abstracting Services with Single Article Provision Services
- Document Provision Brokers and Freelance Information Service Providers

MAIL or *FAX* THIS ENTIRE ORDER FORM TO:

Haworth Document Delivery Service
The Haworth Press, Inc.
10 Alice Street
Binghamton, NY 13904-1580

or FAX: 1-800-895-0582
or CALL: 1-800-429-6784
9am-5pm EST

PLEASE SEND ME PHOTOCOPIES OF THE FOLLOWING SINGLE ARTICLES:
1) Journal Title: _____

   Vol/Issue/Year:_____Starting & Ending Pages:_____
   Article Title:_____

2) Journal Title: _____

   Vol/Issue/Year:_____Starting & Ending Pages:_____
   Article Title:_____

3) Journal Title: _____

   Vol/Issue/Year:_____Starting & Ending Pages:_____
   Article Title:_____

4) Journal Title: _____

   Vol/Issue/Year:_____Starting & Ending Pages:_____
   Article Title:_____

(See other side for Costs and Payment Information)

COSTS: Please figure your cost to order quality copies of an article.

1. Set-up charge per article: $8.00
($8.00 × number of separate articles) _____

2. Photocopying charge for each article:

                          1-10 pages: $1.00 _____

                          11-19 pages: $3.00 _____

                          20-29 pages: $5.00 _____

                          30+ pages: $2.00/10 pages _____

3. Flexicover (optional): $2.00/article _____

4. Postage & Handling: US: $1.00 for the first article/
$.50 each additional article _____

                     Federal Express: $25.00 _____

                     Outside US: $2.00 for first article/
$.50 each additional article _____

5. Same-day FAX service: $.50 per page _____

                         GRAND TOTAL: _____

METHOD OF PAYMENT: (please check one)

❑ Check enclosed ❑ Please ship and bill. PO # _____
(sorry we can ship and bill to bookstores only! All others must pre-pay)

❑ Charge to my credit card: ❑ Visa; ❑ MasterCard; ❑ Discover;
                     ❑ American Express;

Account Number: _____ Expiration date: _____

Signature: ✗ _____

Name: _____ Institution: _____

Address: _____

_____

City: _____ State: _____ Zip: _____

Phone Number: _____ FAX Number: _____

MAIL or *FAX* THIS ENTIRE ORDER FORM TO:

Haworth Document Delivery Service   **or FAX:** 1-800-895-0582
The Haworth Press, Inc.   **or CALL:** 1-800-429-6784
10 Alice Street   (9am-5pm EST)
Binghamton, NY 13904-1580